Partners

Healing From His Addiction

by D. Weiss, Ph.D.

Partners; Healing From His Addiction
Copyright 2001, by Douglas Weiss Ph.D.

Requests for information should be addressed to:

Discovery Press
P.O. Box 51055, Colorado Springs, CO 80949
719-278-3708

Library of Congress Cataloging-in-Publication Data

Weiss, D.
      Partners; Healing from His Addiction/D.W. Weiss, Ph.D.
      p. cm.
      Discovery Press, 2001
      ISBN 1-881292-34-7
      1. Women's Issues 2. Sexuality 3. Sex Addiction
                     00-93584 CIP

Edited by Chere Peterson
Interior designed by Lisa Schaffer
Cover designed by Rod Williamson

Printed in the United States of America

TABLE OF CONTENTS

Chapters

1	Brenda's Story	7
2	Margaret's Story	15
3	Mary's Story	25
4	Kim's Story	35
5	Dora's Story	39
6	Tina's Story	45
7	Miriam's Story	49
8	Low Self Esteem	53
9	Black and White Thinking	61
10	The Need To Control	67
11	Boundaries	73
12	Denial	79
13	Dependence vs. Independence	85
14	Depression	99
15	Food	105
16	Sexual Issues	109
17	Defense Mechanisms	119
18	Me Acting Out?	135
19	Believing Behavior	141
20	The Twelve Steps	147
21	Professional Counseling	181
22	Groups	191

Appendix

A	Support Groups Listings
B	The Twelve Steps
C	Resources
D	Porn Blocker

Introduction

Sexual addiction is growing rampantly across our nation. Men are viewing porn at greater rates than at any other time in history. The affects on our culture because of this growing epidemic of sexual addiction is immeasurable. The silent pain that partners of sex addicts experience day after day because of his addiction has not been unmasked until now.

Over eighty-five women help us compile the most current data on the affects of sex addiction on a partner. The issue of depression is a very common reaction for partners of sexual addicts, and we address their responses in our study. Some of the other issues partners responded to in this book are self esteem, eating disorders and sexuality. *Partners* is the first book to bring you statistical detail from the hearts and lives of these women we call *partners*.

As these partners journey from the devastating affects on their lives from sexual addiction and move on into their own personal recovery program the statistical trail indicates there is much hope as she embarks on her journey toward healing. The results from this research demonstrates that significant progress and healing can be obtained by following a recovery path.

The hope of this book is that any woman in a relationship with a sexual addict can feel that she is not alone in this silent addiction. She can now not only reach out but she can genuinely heal from the affects of his addiction on her life.

Dr. Weiss

1
Brenda's Story

My name is Brenda. I am 36 years old and married to a sex addict. We have been living together now for eight years and were married four years ago. My husband and I met at work; both of us were married (to someone else). Michael presented himself as Mr. Wonderful. His behavior led me to believe he was in love with me. He told me all the right things I wanted and needed (or so I thought), to hear in order to feel celebrated, loved, and wanted. He pursued an adulterous affair with me; I was eager to respond. This affair led me to choose to leave my first husband, who was emotionally abusive and, I believe, a sex addict as well. Michael left his wife, and we moved in with each other.

During our adulterous affair, sex was very connected, passionate, loving and intimate. He treated me like his dream come true: he was kind, gentle, compassionate, patient, and led me to believe that he was a good income earner. Upon moving in with each other, everything changed. I could not put my finger on what the exact problem was. Michael was fired from his job, filed bankruptcy and had very irresponsible spending habits. I resented his obsessive spending (of my money). I financially supported us with my cashed out 401K, savings, credit cards, and current job.

Michael was "an independent contractor" in a business earning NO income! He had a lot of unaccounted for time. He was vague in discussing his whereabouts, and avoided discussion about these issues. He soon introduced pornography into our sexual relationship, stating that it would heighten our sexual satisfaction. I did not want to participate, but went along with it. After all, didn't everyone watch it?

He persuaded me to participate and imitate the sexual activities of the actors. This included sexual devices and books with sex stories for additional fantasy. Sex turned from pleasurable to both mentally and physically painful. I was used in a very degrading, objectifying and painful way. It was a crime against my body and my spirit. When I would not participate, he continued with it, on his own, in secret. He would sneak up in the middle of the night, while I was at work and every time I went out of town, to act out with pornography and masturbate. On many occasions, I confronted him and told him I would not tolerate his behavior. He would apologize and throw out the pornography; then immediately sneak it back in, and the same cycle would repeat itself. It wasn't just the sexual relationship that had now failed. He was emotionally unavailable, controlling, manipulative, and unkind to our children (his son, now 13, my daughter, now 9, both from our previous marriages). He was rude to friends, coworkers, family members, and me. If I was not ready or willing to participate in his sexual desires, he treated me like garbage. In my need to be loved, I would set aside my self-respect and participate, enabling his addiction. I no longer liked anything about him; but I was unable to do anything about it. I was immobilized to the point of going through with marriage to him, unable to say no!

I believed that I was the problem. If I were more physically attractive, lost weight, and worked out, were more mentally stimulating-the list goes on-then he would stop. I compared myself to every attractive woman I saw, whether he was present or not. I checked up on him, looked in his briefcase, wallet, car, fantasized about him acting out, staked out his favorite porno shop, called the video rental for his account activity, and could not sleep at night. I obsessed about him 24 hours a day. I did not realize I had become addicted to him and his behavior. I tried to medicate my pain by "checking out" emotionally and drinking alcohol to avoid feeling the loneliness, emptiness, and desperation. I wanted to just kill the pain. By now I had quit my job and had become financially and emotionally dependent upon him; which is the addict's plan. I had lost my identity, did not know who I was, and most certainly did not like who I had become. I was neglecting my daughter and myself to the extreme. Life continued like this for six years.

After our first wedding anniversary, I confronted Michael with the option of a divorce, so he would be free to pursue his sexual interests. He declared his love for me and that he could give up his inappropriate sexual activities. This was the beginning of a year of him getting better at hiding, more daring in his activities, and my continual drinking of alcohol, obsessing about him, and neglecting my daughter and myself. I began fantasizing about entering into an affair with someone I knew. I imagined that he

9

would love me. I would show Michael that someone saw value in me. I started planning how I would enter into my next adulterous affair. Thankfully, I came to my senses and realized that this was exactly the way I started my relationship with Michael, medicating myself with a man that I believed would love me. I recognized a destructive pattern of my own and chose not to continue in it. In realizing what was happening, I committed to do everything possible in this relationship to bring forth resolution. Meanwhile, his addictive behavior continued getting worse; I would catch him, he would ask for forgiveness, and I would forgive.

He went to counseling for his problem, fooled the counselor, and pacified me. Finally, I recognized that I was at the end of my ability to continue in this addictive, crazy life. I made a decision to purposely catch him in the act so I could kick him out. The opportunity presented itself almost immediately. While I was showering one Sunday morning, in my mind I saw him viewing pornography on the internet and masturbating. I immediately went to verify this. What I had envisioned was accurate to the detail. I told him to get out: he did. This was the true turning point for both of us. I was financially dependent upon him, with an eight year-old daughter and no job! We had no savings or financial assets to speak of. I knew I needed to get help for myself no matter what! I finally . . . after all of this time . . . asked God to help me. And He did . . .

Within days of this event and asking God for help, we were referred to Dr. Doug Weiss, a therapist specializing in sexual addiction. The next week we attended his three-day intensive couples counseling session. This was the moment of truth for both of us. Michael had to face and admit to the fact that his behavior was that of a sex addict. I had to face and admit the fact that I had enabled him all of this time, allowed it to happen, participated, gave empty treats, and was just as much a liar as he. These truths and many more were very difficult for both of us to face. Dr. Weiss helped us to see truths about both of our behavior: he gave us tools to implement immediately that helped change our lives forever.

We both agreed to implement Dr. Weiss's recovery program for sex addicts and partners of sex addicts. I agreed to stay in the relationship conditionally; if he were to act out in his sexual addiction again, the marriage would end. He had become a very good actor and, up to now, lied constantly. I realized I had to learn to believe his behavior, not his words. Dr. Weiss led him to agree to take a polygraph test to prove his truthfulness and sobriety. Thirty days after the intensive counseling session Michael took his first polygraph. He admitted the only reason he had maintained sobriety for the 30 days was because of this polygraph test. The first test revealed he had not disclosed all of sexual activities, such as frequenting strip bars, other sexual partners, including prostitutes, and adult bookstore activities in the sex booths; however, it did prove he had been sober from his sexually addictive behavior for the past 30 days. This was a very bittersweet moment for me. It was painful, yet another, step in the journey. I could accept it, forgive him, and continue forward, or end our marriage now. I chose to continue the journey with him; after all he had been sober for 30 days.

The recovery program included joining support groups, being accountable to each other and the group, working our recovery exercises in Dr. Weiss' books, the Twelve Steps, and learning how to have an intimate relationship. By no means has this been an easy road for us. We have both considered, on more than one occasion, throwing

11

in the towel and calling it quits. We have met one challenge after the next. What has happened, in stopping the sexually acting out activities (which was how he medicated himself for pain), is all of the other behaviors have surfaced: the rudeness, the checked-out frame of mind, manipulation, control, impatience, pouting, pride-destructive behaviors of all kinds. He is diligently working at uncovering the root of, and changing all these behaviors as well.

I have been able to stop consciously enabling him; set boundaries in place and enforce them. The boundaries are for both his behavior and mine. I realize that so much of what I had been doing was feeding his addiction. I am learning to no longer obsess about him, have interests outside of our relationship, and real friendships. The old desperate feeling of not being able to leave him alone, for fear of what he may be doing, has dwindled considerably. I am learning that, if he is going to act out his addiction, he will do it whether I am around or not, and that I can not control him, nor can I change his plans.

I have discovered that, while I blamed everything on him, I did not need to look at any issues I personally have. I truly believed that, if he would just change his behavior, then, indeed, our lives would be wonderful. The truth is that I was not healthy entering into the relationship. I left my husband in my pursuit to be loved and celebrated by a man, believing that sex was the way to find this love. I committed adultery with him and justified myself because everyone does this, and, if my husband treated me right, I wouldn't be participating in this affair. What I have discovered, through working my Twelve Step recovery program, is that if it had not been Michael I left my husband for, it would have been someone else, another sex addict. I needed to look at my own behavior and truly change me. I am now focusing mostly on my own recovery and not as much the recovery of my husband. This is bringing me the peace I have so desired. We are both facilitating Twelve Step recovery groups for sex addiction and partners of sex addicts, using Dr. Weiss's materials. Michael has been sober from his sexual addiction one year and eight months since we went to see Dr. Weiss for the emergency intensive counseling session. He continues to take polygraph tests every 6 months, and we have agreed that he will do this indefinitely. Today our lives are thankfully very different than two years ago. Our financial situation has changed. We now own a house together, have money in savings, and a trading business. We are restoring our relationship with each other, our children and families. All, while reaching out to help others in the same situation. We are just now embarking on discovering what is behind all of these addictive behaviors, accepting these things, and letting God heal us. It has been a long and painful journey, and I believe we are nowhere close to conclusion.

Looking back, I would make the same choice to embark on the journey of recovery together with Michael, my husband, as opposed to separation and divorce. I am truly joyful that we both have committed to recovery and to spiritual growth. I feel better, I like who I am becoming, and am committed to continuing to grow daily. I hope my story will encourage and help you to make the choices you need to be a happier and fulfilled woman.

2
Margaret's Story

*I am an extremely **grateful recovering** spouse of a sex addict/sexual anorexic. I emphasize the words **grateful** and **recovering** because I am infinitely thankful that I found recovery and help for myself regardless of what my husband chose or continues to choose for himself. At first, I could not understand why I needed help and recovery, when it seemed to me that it was my husband who was throwing his life, our marriage, and our family out the window! I thought it was ludicrous that I should be going to counseling and Twelve Step meetings to get help for myself when it was my husband who was addicted to sex and whose acting out, and acting in, was negatively affecting him in emotional, physical, and spiritual ways. Now, gratefully, I understand.*

I now understand that I must have the courage and energy to actively change the things that I can change (and that includes a lot of things), and to keep my nose out of the things I cannot change (especially what my sexually addicted spouse chooses to do or not do). I have given up my former habit of feeling responsible for the choices and actions of other people. I have quieted many of the fears that used to prevent me from living my life to the fullest, that hindered my energy and creativity.

One day, about a year ago, I had one of those moments of divine intervention: I finally accepted that the one thing that I could absolutely, positively, and directly affect and focus my energy on, was my OWN recovery from the negative effects, on me, of my husband's sexual addiction. It was at that moment that a huge burden was lifted from my shoulders. I realized that I would never be alone, in my pain or my joys, because God is running the show – not me, not my sex addicted spouse, not my parents, not my friends and family. It was the start of me actively living my life according to my priorities. I am different now. It's a wonderful, peaceful feeling, and it doesn't go away even when I encounter difficult, or even painful, situations or people. There's that old saying of what doesn't kill us makes us stronger. I am stronger than I was before I went through learning of my husband's sex addiction and from my recovery process. I've learned things about myself, my husband, and about relationships, that I would never have uncovered had I not gone through this process of healing and recovery. There are some people who actually say they are grateful that they went through the experience because of all they've learned from it.

I'm not sure if I can honestly claim that I am grateful that I have gone through this experience, but I can sincerely say that I am in a really good place, at this point in my life, and I am grateful for the knowledge I have gained over the past year and a half. It has been a time of rediscovery for my husband and me as individuals, as well as for us as a couple. I'd like to share my experience with you so that you might find your own place of grace, hope, gentleness, and peace.

I met my husband when I was 23. We dated for four years prior to getting engaged, and were married a year later. We had an amazing relationship. We had common interests in terms of entertainment, spiritual life, social activities, financial goals, and family plans. We communicated well and laughed a lot. We had a high level of respect and trust for one another.

At the time, and even now in retrospect, there were very few, if any, red flags that would have led me to suspect that my husband was a sex addict. He kept his secret world very much hidden from me and from everyone else. Outwardly, he portrayed a persona of a man of integrity and self-confidence. He came across as someone who would never be even remotely interested in pornography, and that he was one of the good guys who would be a sure thing, as far as fidelity and trust were concerned. Outwardly, he appeared to be easygoing, and the kind of person who just didn't let life's pressures bother him.

When I found out about his addiction, it was a complete shock to me – like a bucket of freezing cold water being thrown at my back on a hot, summer day. I was like a deer caught in headlights for months afterwards. I was paralyzed from the shock of finding out that I was married to a man who was so different in reality from the man I thought I had married. I felt alone and afraid, because our first child was a newborn when my husband revealed to me that he was addicted to sex. I was fearful for the future of our family and for our son's relationship with his father.

I was disgusted because of the way that I found out about his addiction. I walked in on him using pornography

17

on the internet in our home office. I felt used and betrayed because I had been taking on nearly all of the responsibility of caring for our newborn child because my husband had told me that things were really hectic at the office, and he needed the extra time at home at night to work. I felt so betrayed when I found out, while I was caring for our son around the clock, and trying to see that my husband had the extra time he needed to focus on work, he was really looking at pornography for hours on end, instead of working. I lost respect and trust in my husband, because even after his initial disclosure of his addiction and his outward signs of a desire to recover (attending Twelve Step meetings, counseling, journaling), he continued to lie to me, and to others about the nature of his acting out behaviors. He still acted-out with pornography, then would lie, and say that he was sober. I felt exhausted, confused, and betrayed, again and again, when I would try to figure out what was the truth, and what was a lie. I would feel guilty for not trusting or believing my husband's words, then would feel foolish and deceived when I would find out that he was lying to me to cover up things he was ashamed of.

I felt anger, sadness, resentment, and loss every day for the first five or six months after finding out about his addiction. I isolated myself from friends and family, for fear that they would find out about my husband's sexual addiction. At first I focused my energies on where he was in his recovery. Was he still acting-out? Was there more to his acting out behaviors that I didn't know about? Was he attending meetings, and being 100% honest with his accountability person and his sponsor? I was exhausting myself, by trying to ensure that he was following all the recommended steps that were needed to recover from this devastating (to both the addict and their family) addiction.

I wanted to do everything I could to ensure that our marriage and family would survive. What I didn't know at the time, is that one of those gifts that I am truly grateful for now, was waiting to reveal itself to me. It was at the moment when I hung up the phone with my doctor telling me that the results of my STD tests, including the test for HIV, were negative, that I received a gift. I realized, at that moment, that I absolutely needed to start taking care of myself, depending on myself and on my spiritual beliefs, not on other people. I realized that this wasn't just a little issue that my husband needed to work through, but that it could have been a death sentence for us and for our newborn son.

I believe he thought I would never find out, and that what I didn't know couldn't hurt me. I also realize now that my husband's addiction, his use of porn, strip clubs, and prostitutes <u>was never, and will never be, a result of something I did or did not do</u>. I don't take it personally. His addiction to porn was not about me or some quality I did not have, but instead was all about him and his self centeredness, lack of self confidence, and anxiety; the thing he had habitually turned to for 25 years, as instant relief from his pain and anxiety about his life.

Long before I met my husband, he was hooked on porn. I just got caught in the cross-fire. It affected me in many ways and caused me much pain and loss. Now I know that it could have been me, or someone else in my shoes, and he would have still been a sex addict. I didn't really believe that until after I had been in recovery for quite a few months. This realization was very important in terms of what I could, and could not, change about our relationship.

*I stopped waiting to see how his sexual addiction recovery was going to unfold. I started focusing on **my** life,* *my happiness, and **my** choices, regardless of where he, or our marriage, ended up. I guess you could say I surrendered the outcome of the situation and started focusing my energies on what I could do each day for myself that would fill my life with smiles, laughter, and love, regardless of whether my husband was choosing a life of sobriety or not. What a freeing feeling! What a gift! I am the only one with the power to directly make my attitude one of happiness, peace, and fulfillment. No one can take that away from me. I realized that I could choose to play the victim, let my circumstances and other people make my choices for me, and to play with my emotions until I was completely devastated – or – I could pick myself back up again, take responsibility for my own happiness, and make active, conscious choices, each day, that are consistent with my values. It was really difficult for me to stop trying to directly affect the outcome of my husband's recovery or the health of our marriage. The interesting thing is that, as I started to live my life with integrity and with 100% responsibility for my own choices and my happiness, it started to positively influence (I now understand the HUGE difference between influencing someone and trying to change or control someone) my spouse, our marriage, and my relationships with others.*

*I also used to take on much shame and guilt on myself for the acting-out behaviors of my husband. I felt ashamed of him because of the kinds of behaviors he did when acting out his addiction. I felt ashamed to be associated with him or to have my friends and family discover the truth of my husband's acting out behaviors. Now, fortunately, I understand that I do not have to take on shame or to feel guilty for **his** actions and **his** choices. Those are **his** choices, not mine. I also understand now that, just because*

I choose to stay in the marriage does not mean that I like or condone his past acting-out behaviors. I used to think I had to take some drastic action, like separation or divorce, to show him how much I disliked the things he did. I felt that I had to take some action to respond to the hurt he had caused me. Now I know that this is not true. Sometimes, the best thing to do has been to do absolutely nothing at all and to just have patience, compassion, and humility. When I surrender the responsibility for the actions of other people, I also release myself from feeling ashamed for the consequences of their actions. It is extremely freeing!

It was very powerful when I recognized that I have a choice as to whether I stay and work on my marriage, or whether I choose to leave the marriage. At first, I had told myself that if I just read enough self-help books on sexual addiction, went to counseling, went to meetings, worked the Twelve Steps, did marital counseling, and my husband got and stayed sober, that our marriage would be all but guaranteed to weather the storm of sexual addiction. I had not given myself permission to even consider the possibility of divorce. I was too afraid, ashamed, angered, and prideful to allow myself to even consider the possibility that my husband might choose to continue practicing his addiction, and that our marriage might not survive.

I did not accept at that time that I, alone cannot make a healthy, intimate marriage or relationship with another person. It was another gift for my peace of mind when I realized that, even though I couldn't directly control the outcome of our marriage or my husband's recovery, that I did have the power to choose whether or not to staying the marriage. When I realized I could choose whether or not to fall into the victim role, and that I was not trapped at gunpoint in the marriage, this was extremely powerful and freeing for me. I finally realized that if my husband did in fact continue practicing his addiction, I could choose to end the marriage. I hadn't let myself consider that option. I hadn't accepted the fact that I couldn't directly affect the outcome of my husband's recovery from sexual addiction. This realization really forced me to look at my wants, needs, desires, and dreams rather than focus on what my husband was doing.

One of the realizations I had that was key to my recovery, was that I had been, moment-by-moment, creating the path out of the wreck that our marriage was a year and a half ago. At first, I just assumed that there was a right and a wrong way to recover from sexual addiction and now my husband's addiction affected me. I grew up in an alcoholic home. My father was an active alcoholic until I was a teenager. He's been sober for twenty plus years and very active in Twelve Step recovery programs. The drinking stopped, but the crazy, negative dynamics in my parents' marriage have never been effectively addressed. They are both very unhappy and unfulfilled in their marriage today, yet they stay married.

It was important for me to realize that I have the power to make different choices and to take a different path than my role models. My husband's parents' marriage ended in divorce and he has a lot of fears related to that as well. It was key when he and I both realized that we did not have to follow the paths that we have observed in our lives. We can create a new path that works for us and our circumstances. We realize that this is not an easy path to choose – it requires a boatload of patience, humility and spirituality. It really changed my perspective on the relationship and affected the way I communicate with my husband. I became much more direct and much more assertive in communicating my wants, needs, and desires to my husband, and he has also opened up to me in these areas. I realized that marriage is truly a two-way street: both partners need to give 100% to the relationship and to rediscover each other. In many ways, I feel as if my husband and I are starting over in a new relationship. We have both changed in so many ways that it is like we are recreating our marriage every day. We know each other on such a deeper level than ever before. Recovery hasn't been easy at times but I am grateful so far. My story is mine and I hope you take your power to create your own story of your life regardless of your spouse's choices.

3
Mary's Story

My name is Mary. I am 47 years old. I am a teacher, but during my marriage, I was a stay-home mom helping my husband in his self-employed business. I have three children ages 9 (boy), 13 (girl), and 16 (girl).

I met "John" in 1981; we were married in 1983; separated in 1997; and divorced in December 1999. John is the only sex addict I have ever known, or perhaps more correctly, identified. I don't believe that I ever had a relationship with anyone else with this problem.

I believe that I was emotionally abused by my mother. The only significance of this is that the behavior that I learned as a child seemed normal to me as an adult. The feelings of failure, responsibility, and disappointment were all normal feelings for me in a relationship. I didn't feel worthy as a child, therefore, when I didn't feel worthy as a wife/mother—I felt the responsibility was mine. I was to blame.

Unfortunately, I showed my hand so early to him (my desire to marry a spiritual man), that he was able to manipulate my feelings very easily. The first time we had sex was on a Saturday night. He took me to his church Sunday morning. Who couldn't love a guy who would have that much respect for me—at least that was what I thought. I also had decided that his almost insecure behavior, was really extreme confidence. He had a very successful atti-tude, with a wonderful laugh, a highly romantic (though manipulative) side, and people really seemed to like him (on first impression). Money didn't seem to be an issue with him, and since it was for me, I loved the idea that he appeared to be in confident control.

*I became aware of John's attraction to pornography when we were still dating. During the first few months of our relationship, I realized that John was not being totally honest with me some of the time. He was receiving phone signals from someone when he said that he wasn't emotion-ally attached to anyone. (Ring once, ring twice). I went out to the street to get his mail a couple of times, and found letters from a woman. (He had recently moved from another state, and the letters were from that state. They were scented). As I became curious, I began to look around his house, drawers, closets. I found opened letters from an-other woman, unopened letters from this other woman and his mother. I thought the unopened letters were strange. I also found **Penthouse** and **Hustler** magazines in his bed-side table. I had never seen a Hustler before, and I found it to be repulsive. This scared me. I also found other things that I related to sexual activity. By this time, we had be-come sexual, but I decided that he was probably just a lonely, single man with normal needs.*

*As I settled into our relationship, the things that bothered me were the **Hustler**, the phone signals and the lying. He treated me well, as long as I didn't challenge him.*

When I questioned him about things, that was when I felt that he was lying to me—to make himself look better. I just decided that this was dating stuff, and that he wanted me to see him in the best light. When I finally became concerned enough to want more answers, I steamed open a couple of unopened letters from the other woman. That was when I had confirmation of the phone signals, her frustrations that he wasn't returning the signal, and the depth of his relationship with this other woman. They definitely still had a relationship, and now he had me too. I was too ashamed of my snooping to challenge him with what I knew, but with more information, his lies were more obvious.

*The pornography seemed to disappear, and eventually, so did the other woman. A year-and-a-half later, we married. The lying was still a small problem, but no porn. It didn't return until I was pregnant with our second child. I just thought that John was having trouble adjusting to my "ugliness". It appeared innocently as **Victoria Secret** catalogues. Then, one day, when I thought I was turning on a video tape that I had recorded, I was shocked to see a porn movie where "General Hospital" was supposed to be. I felt shocked, hurt, disappointed, ugly, betrayed, and ashamed. I pretended that I hadn't found the tape. I hid my pain, and continued on like normal.*

Over the course of the next year, I began to recognize changes in our relationship, and was able to put some perspective on things. When I returned home from errands (he worked out of our home), and could see that I had surprised him (this happened many times), I quickly learned that I was interrupting his porn sessions. He was obviously masturbating, the evidence being the lotion that kept disappearing from my dressing table and reappearing on his bedside table. I started snooping again and found several video tapes hidden in his closet.

The changes in the relationship mostly came in the form of his rages. The pattern became porn-rage. I could always tell that he had been watching videos because he was irrationally angry. This continued for over a year, and I never said anything. I had the need to leave the house, and stay home at the same time. It didn't seem to matter what happened in our sex life, the porn didn't go away. We had sex at least once a day, in addition to his porn activity. I felt that I was unable to satisfy him, and my self-esteem quickly started to descend.

I started making excuses for him regarding the things that I knew to be true. He had another girlfriend in another state, and lied about things surrounding her.

My self esteem was getting very low. Other people pointed this out to me. I started to pull away from my friends because I was ashamed. I was living a lie, and I knew it. Also, our friends began to notice changes in him, and they didn't like it.

Depression was real. I became pregnant with our third child. I felt that I was trying very hard to help John overcome some of the things that I had noticed were problems, but nothing I seemed to do would help. The porn would come and go, according to his mood, and his level of discouragement. It was a drug to him.

One time, I actually took the video out of the machine when I found it, and put it on top of the TV. I was hoping that he would see that I was on to him, but it didn't seem to matter. Our fights were more frequent, and more emotionally painful. I never, ever told him "No" to sex. I thought I was helping. I finally decided to tell his best friend, our church pastor, and together we talked to John. He was outraged, extremely angry, and felt betrayed by me. He denied his activity at first, but then admitted it. He said there wasn't anything wrong with what he was doing; it was normal. He was actually offended that he couldn't get our pastor to agree with him. After our pastor left, John became remorseful, went into the bedroom, brought two video tapes to me, and we both walked outside and threw them into the garbage. He said that he didn't know that it was hurting me so much. This was one point where I realized the trouble that I was in, because, about 15 minutes later, I secretly went out the back door, went to the trash can, removed the tapes and pulled the tape out of the cassette. I realized that I didn't believe John, or trust him.

Bottom came about five years later. The porn had slowly returned. The lying was becoming bigger, and I found out through my fine-tuned snooping skills, that John was having what appeared to be an affair. When I had gathered enough evidence, I confronted him. He denied. Through this process, I had again shown my hand, and many of my avenues of snooping were cut off. I no longer had access to our post office box—John took my key. He often took money, credit cards, etc. away from me in an attempt to control me. By keeping me from having access to phone bills, and credit card bills, John made it more difficult for me to keep track of his activities. That girl disappeared. Within six months, there were signs again, and I snooped. I got very skilled at snooping, and by now, his addiction had convinced him that I was stupid. I let stupid work for me.

With the appearance of girlfriend #2, I confronted him again, but this time I was very careful as to the evidence that I gave him. I didn't want him to cut me off of my sources, so I "manipulated" the information that I gave him. He knew that he had been busted, and said that he *would give her up (along with the denial that it wasn't a sexual relationship—she just cut his hair a couple of times).*

I managed to get through Christmas, with the evidence that she was not gone, then I skillfully left him for three days. I had support of some key people, since leaving a man like John is a scary thing. I was feeling very power-less, unless I had things structured correctly. I had to remove him from my credit card, just so he couldn't remove me from it. I took the kids, and communicated with him (and his mother, pastor, and another friend) by phone. I demanded that we go to marriage counseling, that he move his office out of our home (I was trying to get him to grow-up), and that girlfriend #2 go away. After three days, I felt that he was sincere enough to return home. My kids didn't know what we were doing, just that it was a mini-vacation. I thought this was the bottom, but it wasn't.

Within four months, the girlfriend was back. To cover himself, he locked me out of his inner office where he had relocated his business to. During his relocation, I found a recorder that he had been using to tape all of my phone calls. I didn't let him know that I found it, but I realized that he knew who I was relying on for emotional support. All of those friends were shut down by him. He wouldn't even allow me to use the phone, or pass callers/messages on to me. He began to tell my friends that I wasn't home. I was very relieved when he moved the office out, since it gave me a little more freedom at home. It took me three long days of searching to find a key to his inner office. He still needed me to do work, but didn't allow me to have access to his inner sanctum. Once I found the key, I began to find lots of evidence of his activities. It was then that I realized that he was very emotionally involved with this girl.

Our marriage counseling wasn't going well because John couldn't be honest. After a year of counseling, our counselor told us that he couldn't help us. I began to hear programs on the radio letting me know that I was not alone. Of course, with the office, he had even more freedom, and was coming home even later. I had less of a watch on him, but was actually more relaxed. Knowing that he was having a sexual affair made our sex a terrible thing. He continued to want to have sex everyday, and I wasn't ready yet to confront him about his affair. He thought he was fooling me, and I allowed him to think that. Sex had become emotionally painful—like I would imagine a rape to feel. I even began to dig my fingernails into the palm of my hands in order to help my mind locate on another part of my body (Lamaze thinking). The pain in my hands kept me from thinking about the sexual pain.

One night, his father stopped into his office when he saw the lights on (about 9:00 P.M.). His Dad walked in to the office to find John and his girlfriend sitting on the office couch. This was the break I needed to confront the situation. His mother called me to tell me, and John came home within ten minutes—to explain. It took me another six months dealing with the situation, the counseling, then finding a lawyer, and filing for a legal separation. This was the bottom. As an unemployed mother, I had nothing. As a controlling man, he wouldn't give me anything. He was so angry at my betrayal of him, that it turned ugly very fast. He wanted me to go to counseling, with another counselor that he trusted, so we did that. It took her about one year to get his number, so we left there. We went to a third counselor, but he told John, point-blank, that this wouldn't help until John decided to be honest. (This only took four months). During this time, the girlfriend disappeared, but several other women appeared; after all, we were separated. After a total of three counselors, and three or four girlfriends, I finally filed for divorce. He wasn't willing to give up the porn, and I wasn't willing to live with it.

I withdrew from my support groups, since the first thing I had to do with the legal separation was to get a job. I was also too ashamed to be with people. We had been very involved with our church, and I was embarrassed about my situation. It has taken me a couple of years to be able to reach out to people again. My counseling is the only thing that has kept me on the road to recovery. (I stayed with counselor number two). I have read several books, and learned a lot about the behavior that was surrounding me for so many years. I learned how I played a part in this dysfunctional relationship. I learned that the problem wasn't me.

Sexual addiction is like a drug. The drug is covering up pain. The pain is within the addict. I have learned that honesty in a relationship is the most essential part. Without the trust that goes with honesty, the relationship is a lie. I have learned that pornography is progressive. It grows and moves within the addict. It is powerful enough to cause severe personality changes that are destructive to any relationship. I have learned that it is contagious, since it creates a fantasy world in the mind of the addict, and affects parenting to the point of danger.

John would never, and still cannot, admit that pornography is a problem. Without awareness of that truth from him, the relationship had no chance of survival. We divorced. Our relationship now, as two people trying to parent our children is horrible. He still is angry, to the point of hate, and thinks of me as the one who betrayed him. He refuses to cooperate. The divorce was long and painful. I got out of the marriage with very little, since he could afford a good lawyer, and I couldn't. He managed to hide most of our assets from the court, and I was powerless to do anything about it. I got to the point that I just wanted out. I have now been divorced for 3 years. My children used to see me as the problem, since I initiated the divorce. But, since John's behavior has not gotten any better, as my kids get older, they have begun to see the problems. Exposure to sexuality, lying, raging, and emotional battering of their Mom, has left all three of my kids with enough awareness, that survival is their game. The pain of the truth puts them into denial much of the time. We have joint custody- one week/one week. He has the money to bribe, entertain, travel, etc. I have the love to make it all right. I am their anchor.

4
Kim's Story

*My name is Kim. I met my husband in the 7th grade.
At first I didn't like him. I thought he was arrogant and
elusive. By the ninth grade I changed my mind about him.
All of a sudden he was mysterious, funny, and a little on the
edge. Maybe I wanted the challenge of taming him. I think
my very strict up bringing begged for someone to unlock
things for me. I knew he seemed a little dangerous, but
what did I have to lose at sixteen? Right from the start sex
was definitely not acceptable. That was until two years went
by and he said it was time we really had sex because oral,
finger masturbation, and partial penetration weren't really
sex. I felt stupid. Being a virgin and staying that way meant
a lot to me. This went on for about three years. Our relationship was full of fights. He was angry a lot and I always
felt it was something I could have done differently. We
decided to move in together. This was against my parents
wishes. We had lots of pressure and no help from family. He*

worked nights, and I worked days. We decided for our wedding we would abstain. We lasted until the night before the wedding. I remember thinking after we were done "Tomorrow it will be beautiful." This is what I had heard from my mother. It was similar to the story of a butterfly. Before marriage, sex is ugly and it will eat up everything in your life. Then your honeymoon night, it is the most beautiful thing you could ever imagine. The magic cocoon of our wedding bed didn't change a thing, in fact it got worse. He was gone all the time working, hunting, or playing with friends. It was convenient that I was always there when he needed me. Our sex life was great I thought. What I was comparing it to I don't know. I thought it was normal to feel used afterward. I took pride in being sexy and being good at it. My whole persona was wrapped in this thinking. The more he liked me in bed, the more he liked the way I looked, the happier we would be. I even had three children to try and fix our marriage. I made enough money to get him out of his job. He bought every imaginable toy a man could own. Still, he stayed volatile, critical, harsh, and distant.

I learned to stay lonely while never being alone. If we had problems, I knew it was only me. I took the blame and enjoyed the challenge of fixing it. Just when I thought I had figured it out, again, our life was a mess. At the end of twelve years of marriage, a bottle of wine a night wasn't helping anymore either. We had tried it all, from swinging, to counseling, and still no peace. I remember the day I found out who my husband really was. He was everything my deepest, darkest dream could conjure up. A sly con-man, and a liar, who cared of nothing else than other . women to play with. He was never satisfied with me or the many others. I realized this after one of his affairs while I

*was pregnant with my fourth child. He was with my best
friend in my house, and I never knew it. I justified it, and
said, "well he made a mistake." So I packed us up and we
moved to a new state where no one knew us. Somewhere I
could walk down the street and not remember his mistake.
Four months in our new improved life, I caught him on the
internet porn sites talking with women. I knew then there
was more than one affair. We had a problem. That was
the start of uncovering the hurt and pain. The twelve years
of affairs with many friends and acquaintances made this
one minimal. The polygraph he had to take revealed it all,
and he felt free. I felt assaulted, raped, and left for dead.
That was a year ago. He was diagnosed and treated for
sexual addiction. I learned what that meant and I learned I
had issues, too.*

*In recovery, I found it difficult to have my needs meet.
My husband was so busy keeping his act together, that there
was nothing left over for me. I reached out to spirituality to
fill in the gaps in my needs. I was tired of the whole thing.
At times I hated talking about it. It was, and still is, frustrating to go into public. I catch myself wondering what is
going on in his mind. It took me almost nine months to feel
comfortable in a public place with him. This was a big
issue for me to overcome. I would cry a lot in recovery, too.*

*We learned to have intimate sex, and this was scary. I
guess all of those years I was used to not having my needs
met. It was difficult to receive real love and appreciation.
We are happy sex doesn't rule our lives. We think of it as
icing on the cake. We do it when we feel like it, and we are
intimate in a lot of other ways. We talk a lot, and I don't
feel like an outsider anymore. There are times in my recovery when I feel him slipping away. I have learned to let him
deal with his own stuff. I focus on treating him like I want*

to be treated with no expectations or a check list. This has really released anxiety for the both of us. I tell him what I need, before I am starved for it.

Recently the saying I learned in my Twelve Step group, "letting go and letting God" has helped me a lot on going forward. Most of all it has freed me of being his mother, baby-sitter, or warden. The biggest challenge in it all was living out all the consequences of what he had done. We lost everything material as well as our status. I think of it as a blessing now. We were stripped of everything. It was there that we found the freedom in what really matters. We are living and loving today, and happy with it. I am excited about helping other women and families broken by the affects of sexual addiction. If we made it, so can you. There is hope, you just have to decide to beat it. My hope is that many receive recovery from the affects of this addiction. There is great strength and power in recovery to make a difference for others.

5
Dora's Story

Hello and welcome to my story. I am an incest survivor, an adult child of alcoholics, and oh yeah, a recovering partner to a recovering sex addict. I write this in hopes that it will give those in the same situation the courage to face their issues and to know they are precious in every way. Life for me is better now, but it hasn't always been that way. At twenty-one, I could no longer deny that my childhood and the way I was brought up had greatly affected who I was and the choices I made. It would be six years from then that I would enter recovery. Recovery from my life.

The incest is a very important part of my life, but it no longer has power over me. I don't think my older cousin knew the damage he was doing when he molested me. He was a teenager at the time and I was around six years old. This happened off and on for a few years and luckily never reached intercourse. In addition to stealing my innocence, the incest stole a lot of my childhood memories. It also implanted the wrong beliefs about sex, love and trust. The beliefs that would later find me married to a sex addict.

Now, being the child of alcoholics would also prepare me quite well for the role of a partner, not just to a sex addict, but to anything that breathed. I am the youngest of three, all of whom have different fathers. My older sister, by ten years, raised me a great deal of the time, because my parents worked a lot and were helping my grandparents as well. I also have an older brother, but he was always with his friends and of little help. I do remember some great times with the family, and I will always cherish those memories. I love my parents a great deal to this day; they did the best they could with what they knew. We always had everything we needed and were never hungry. There was just one problem, they were weekend alcoholics and were teaching me how to be the perfect caretaker. When my siblings married and left home, it was my turn to take care of my parents and see to it that they got into the house safely and into bed. This was a common routine on weekends for a small ten year old, who was not going to be able to stop a drunk adult from falling on the porch. I hated their drinking and hated how embarrassing they were.

When I was fourteen, my father died of liver cancer. I withdrew inside and dealt with my pain alone. My father was a kind, loving, and patient man. In fact, he never ever hit any one of us kids. My mother had always been the screamer and impatient parent. Her words could do more damage than if she just hit you. His death destroyed both me and my mother and sent her into a deeper abyss of alcohol. This time it was every day, and she was going out a lot.

By sixteen, I was totally obsessed with a guy who

*dumped me because I wouldn't have sex with him. I felt
rejected and abandoned because sex means love. It was
okay, because I immediately found someone else to latch
onto. Too bad he was too healthy and there just wasn't
anything to fix. After three years of being with him and
giving myself to him, I had to go out and mess it all up. Get
this, I went out and cheated on him with the guy who
dumped me all those years back.*

 *I realize now it was all me who ruined that relation-
ship. It didn't take me long to cling to the next person who
showed me obsessive attention. He turned out to be the sex
addict in my life, and the person I am truly grateful for. I
believe we are gifts to one another. In spite of all the pain
this person has caused, he helped me realize I was worth
finding my true self and resolving all issues of the past.
Today, I no longer want to control, caretake, or obsess.*

 *At the time, I didn't know exactly who I was falling in
love with, but I should have run the other way when he
tried to make out with me and my girlfriend, on the same
day we met. I didn't run away, because I saw a wounded
soul needing to be fixed and saved, <u>my specialty</u>. We married within a year, and I transferred universities to live
where my husband worked. I was twenty and he was twenty-
five. At first, the strip clubs, porn videos, and magazines
didn't bother me. I had grown up thinking this was normal
guy stuff, and, as long as they weren't really cheating on
you, it was okay. Plus, I was trying to be this cool wife, up
with the times. Little did I know I was slowly giving my soul
away and permitting him to disrespect me. After I found a
phone call record to his ex-fiancee, I knew I had made a
grave mistake in marrying this person. I felt so betrayed
and alone, but I knew I couldn't go back to my mother, who
was against the marriage from the beginning.*

Once again, I was filled with shame and embarrassment. I soon began having flashbacks of the incest, which made sex with my husband disgusting. I wouldn't have sex for fear of the incest memories, which caused many fights because sex was the most important thing to my husband. My husband knew of the incest but not of the flashbacks. I often disconnected during sex and left my body. Finally, I just couldn't take the feelings of disgust and darkness anymore. Even then, a part of me knew I deserved better and was worth so much more. These powerful emotions gave me the courage to tell my husband no more porn magazines in my home. We fought, I won. Then came strip clubs. We fought, I won. At least, it was like that on the surface.

My husband and I had so many great times, but we weren't really happy. In fact, I was miserable and wanted out of my marriage, but my fear of abandonment kept me there. It wasn't until I almost accidently killed myself handling an unsafe gun, that I realized I was not living a quality life. The doctor said I should have died. Even though this scared my husband, it wasn't enough for him to see what I saw. He continued in his addiction, porn, strip clubs, fantasy and masturbation. In the meantime, I sought counseling, because I thought I was the problem and it was time to deal with my past.

My husband refused to go with me, which meant he didn't love me enough. That was okay, the healthier I got, the clearer my mind became to his problem. Before I knew it, I was dealing with the Queen of Seduction, the Internet. It was in my home and had a tight grip on my husband. I remember feeling so hopeless, I still didn't have a name to his problem. I truly began to think I wasn't good enough and that my husband was cheating on me. I spent a lot of time and energy trying to make me look better. By this time, I was so afraid of infidelity that I allowed him to look at body parts and porn on the Internet.

I was expecting our first child and really had just given up on my husband. He was full of lies and empty promises that I kept falling for. After our son was born, and while in one of my searching binges, I found his secret stash of favorite porn on our computer. I was disgusted and physically sick to find teen websites. I totally lost it and raged for days, something my mother taught me well. I was scared that I had married a child molester. He promised to stop looking at porn on the internet, but he failed. One night, I caught him talking to another woman on the computer, the one rule we were never to break. I raged and threatened to leave him, which I got good at, but he once again convinced me it wasn't sexual in nature. It was very difficult, because I didn't want to believe the person I loved, and who was supposed to love me in return, could hurt me this way. I was wrong.

One day upon returning from a trip with my son, I sensed something very wrong in the house. I immediately went to his computer and discovered a deleted e-mail. It was a very detailed letter to a woman describing how wonderful she made him feel. My heart and soul died at that moment. I began having an anxiety attack and couldn't breathe. The anger quickly took over. While my mother watched our son in the next room, I confronted my husband in our bedroom. I accused him of cheating. He denied ever doing that, which lucky for him he was telling the truth. No matter, the scene was pathetic, and I was completely destroyed. It was the worst feeling I had ever felt, the painful slap to reality I could no longer deny. I left my husband on that day, with no intentions of coming back. There were no more tears.

He sought help and discovered the name to his problem, sex addiction. Together, we have been in recovery for a year and a half now and have been in counseling. We try to work our Twelve Steps to the best we can and be gentle with ourselves at the same time. We know what true intimacy is and are slowly putting ourselves back together.

The road is not always easy, and we have our moments, but we have people to call now. Through this journey, I am learning to take responsibility for my choices and feelings, past and present. The guilt and shame have very little power over me, and I truly love myself now. Also, my inner child knows that she can trust me to always keep her safe. Today, I know I am a precious gift and look forward to this journey of new self discovery. I can now say I am worth my recovery and mean it!

6
Tina's Story

I am in my mid-30's, my now ex-husband is ten years older than me. I am an artist; he works in the engineering field. We both had never been married before and have no children.

After 5 years of marriage to a sex addict I finally divorced him this past March. He chose not to ever admit that he had a problem. His acting out behaviors (that I know about) are voyeurism and a pornography addiction.

His specialty is using the video camera to spy on women, particularly at the beach, and through windows and fences. He also has a collection of videos of other girlfriends and himself having sex. I never allowed him to videotape me nude or during sex — yet he did so without my knowledge anyway. His collection of pornography was very large - maybe a few hundred tapes or more. I once asked him why he needed so many tapes and he told me, "because I like to see different women's bodies".

Partners

When I first married him I thought that his collection of porn was a little excessive, but I knew nothing about sex addiction and did not give it too much thought. I figured that a man that had not been married and was 40 years old was lonely a lot or something.

After we were married he insisted that porn be on the television every time he and I had sex. I was not happy with this at all, but at the time I felt trapped without any job or money of my own. He took control of all our finances. When we got married, we had moved out of state for a job promotion for him.

I knew something was wrong right away when (very early in our marriage), he would not want to have sex with me, yet I would catch him masturbating to porn late at night after I had gone to sleep. After a while he would no longer have intercourse with me at all. He would only want me to give him oral sex while he watched porn on the TV. During this time we fought a lot about sex. In fact, it was really the only thing we did fight about. I stupidly went along with this for about a year.

My self-esteem plummeted. I knew something was really wrong, but I first blamed myself. I became very depressed. I thought it was because I had gained five pounds, or that I was not in as good of shape as when I met him.

After the first year of marriage, we moved back to our home state. I found a job that I was very happy with, and I was closer to my friends and family. My husband and I were busy remodeling our dream house. I put my efforts into this and my job. It was at this time that I had enough of the porn! I put all his porn tapes in a big lawn bag and drove away, later dumping them in a dumpster outside of a store. I went to stay the night at his parents house. I *returned the next day to find many of my personal belonging missing or destroyed. He did apologize later, but things became worse and worse. That weekend he even woke up talking in his sleep about his missing video tapes. He was obviously very distraught about losing them. I was happy that I no longer had to see them any more!*

After that he would still want the TV on during his once a week blow job. He would watch anything. He liked to have the remote in his hand — changing channels. Without this he would take forever to climax or could not at all. We had intercourse once in the last four years of my marriage — on a vacation. He told me not to get use to it because "it was vacation sex." I went in the bathroom afterward and cried. It was at this time that he also became physically violent towards me.

One day at work I saw something about sexual addiction in an article. I looked for more information. I was thrilled, I thought that maybe there would be a way to "fix" the problem if I could show my husband this information. I sat down with him and tried to talk to him about it. I showed him articles and things about sexual addiction. He became extremely angry. At the time, I did not know about my co-dependency behaviors. I thought that I could find some way of fixing him. I thought at the time, "at least I know that there was not something wrong with me."

I tried many ways to cope with his sex addiction. Finally I realized that I could not stay in the marriage and be happy. He was never going to get help or even admit he had any problem. I was sick of living without sex and intimacy. I filed for divorce and a restraining order.

He was horrible during the divorce proceedings. Even though, I still miss him. I am also glad that I do not have to live with these behaviors any more. I am sad that he refused to get any help and allowed it to destroy our marriage.

7
Miriam's Story

My name is Miriam. I'm 35 years old. I've been married for seven years. No children yet. When I first met my husband, I knew at that moment that he was the one. We started to get to know each other, and a month later he proposed to me. I said yes. Everything was so perfect and beautiful. We dated for nine months, and then we married. Everything seemed normal for a while until my husband decided to quit his job (he was working nights) to start his own business (Multi-Level Marketing). At the time I agreed because I knew that he could not deal with the night shift.

So the journey starts. The first six months he was not making any money. Tension begins. Then I started to nag him. I wanted him to get a job. He did not like me to tell him what to do. More tension. By then our sexual intimacy was being affected. Less and less sex. I started to have battles in my mind. I asked myself, what is going on? Why isn't he approaching me? Maybe because I gained weight? Or maybe because I am not pleasing him the way he likes it? I knew he was not having an affair because most of the time we were together. So what was it? I also remember that he had porn tapes in the house. I started to check up on him. I had my suspicions about him looking at these tapes. Another woman, who is now my friend, accountability person and sponsor, was going through her healing process after she discover that her husband was a sex addict and came into my life. She told me many things and she taught me about how pornography can affect a marriage.

Everything that I was learning I would tell my counselor but it seemed that she did not believe me. This was the first time I heard there was such a thing called sexual addiction. My understanding was that all men looked at pornography and that it was good for a relationship. I was so wrong. I was married before, but I know that my ex-husband did not have a problem like this one because we had a healthy sexual life. He did not like to watch porn, because he said those things were faked. That we could do better than that. My marriage failed because of adultery. No one knew what the real problem was.

Then when I was about to lose hope, I tried my last chance. I spoke to my senior pastor. I told him what I knew. He listened. Then he said he needed to hear my husband's side of the story. I finally started to see the light. Not only that I knew that my husband had problems, I also discovered that I had big time problems too. I discovered that I was an adult child of an alcoholic, I am co-dependent, I had low-self esteem and no boundaries. I decided that I wanted to work on my issues. At that point I took the focus away from my husband and started to work on myself. I wanted to get well and healthy.

Three months later an incident happened. I went to bed and my husband decided that he was going to check his e-mail. I fell asleep. Around an hour later I heard this soft voice that said "get up, get up." My mind started running and also my heart. I said, please let it not be what I think it is. But unfortunately it was. I caught my husband looking for pornography on the Internet. That was when my whole world went down. It was confirmed to me that my husband is a sex addict. At that moment he could not deny it. He finally confessed. I told him a week later that if he did not get help in this area within three months that I would want a separation. He became rebellious and decided not to get help.

So, on our fifth wedding anniversary, I moved out. I had to do it, because I couldn't focus on my issues if he wasn't doing the same. I needed the space. And I'm glad I did that. We were separated for 16 months. The first six months, I focused on my spirituality. Then I joined a support group, a safe place to talk about my issues. I had to face the reality that I was sexually abused as a child (one of my uncles). In that group there was a recovered sex addict and every time he would speak, it gave me so much encouragement. He also helped me understand what a man goes through when they have this addiction. He always used to say to me that I was not the problem. I continued professional counseling. My healing process was beginning. Then my husband and I started to talk more often and spend more time together. He finally came out of his denial. He started to look for help. Finally some light at the end of the tunnel.

On December 25th we decided to reconcile, and I came back home. Today my husband is working in his recovery process and also facilitating a support group for men struggling with sexual addiction; he has not acted-out for the last eight months. Remember the man in the support group? He is my husband's mentor. We're still in the healing process. Our sex life has improved somewhat but not totally. In my story there is sexual anorexia. But I know now there is hope for me and for all of the women out there that are just discovering this addiction.

8
Low Self Esteem

Low self-esteem is an issue for many partners of sex addicts. The clinical community has agonized over this issue for more than a decade. It is common for clinicians to hear statements from partners of sex addicts reflecting their low self esteem. Some of these statements are printed below.

- Who will love me now?
- I can't do anything.
- I'm so unattractive.
- I don't even like Me anymore.
- No man would want me now.

I could fill the pages of an entire book with the list of statements from partners sharing how valueless they feel.

In a recent survey of partners of sex addicts, we asked several questions about self-esteem. The results of these findings may help put into perspective what happened to the self-esteem many partners of sex addicts *used to have*.

Prior to my relationship with the sex addict, I felt my self-esteem was:

> 25% High
> 40% Average
> 27% Low
> 08% Very low

During my relationship with the sex addict, I felt my self-worth was:

> 05% High
> 20% Average
> 38% Low
> 37% Very low

Let's look at these statistics next to each other so you can see the impact that living with a sex-addict has on a partner. This affect on the self esteem is on the majority of partners of sex addicts. Few partners go unaffected in this area of esteem by the disease of sexual addiction.

	Before	During	Difference
High	25%	05%	-20%
Average	40%	20%	-20%
Low	27%	38%	+09%
Very Low	08%	37%	+29%

The affects of sexual addiction on the self-esteem of

a partner are obvious. Some partners had low self-esteem prior to the relationship with an addict. Addicts can easily spot a woman with low self-esteem. This is an easy victim for the sex addict.

In this situation, he lavishes you with praise and tells you how wonderful you are. He says you do everything right and tells you how smart you are. He'll also say what a good lover you are early in the relationship. This is to shift your self-esteem onto what he thinks about you. This is enjoyable for a while, but, often soon after marriage, you quickly find out that he now has your self-esteem in his hands. Now you may not be so wonderful. It feels like you can do little right, and your self-esteem plummets even lower as the addict seeks more control of your thoughts and beliefs about yourself.

Another case in point is where the partner begins with average to high self-esteem. In this case, it often takes the sex addict longer to lower the self-esteem. A change may need to be made in where you live. He may ask you to leave your job, so that he can be at home with you more. He will try other ways to remove you from some of the external stability, where you will become more isolated. Then there are the continual overtones that you are not as sexy as you once were. You are now "gaining a little weight." He will focus on a body part of yours until you question your value. This can be combined with the nagging to do other types of sexual behaviors, that you are not comfortable with and not acceptable to you. You may be called a prude as the addict tries to engage you in his world and chip away at your self-esteem.

He may now begin looking at other women. Partners tell me every time their addict looks at someone else with "those eyes" they feel less of a woman. Finding pornography of unclad models can contribute to a partner feeling "less than."

Partners of sex addicts frequently say they don't feel good about themselves. They experience what clinicians call low self-esteem. This is a feeling that, "I am not as good as, or not equal to, other people I know." In their relationships, these partners feel "less than" or "one down" from the sex addict they are dating or married to.

Often the truth is, people are attracted to partners with self-esteem similar to their own. Sex addicts are usually trying to increase their sense of value through their addiction. At the core of the sex addict is their belief that, "if they really knew me, they wouldn't love me."

The feeling of being unworthy of love because of who she is as partner to a sex addict instead of what she does, is also part of her low self-esteem. Most significant, though, is her belief that her value lies in being "enough" for the sex addict.

We live in a culture where we are encouraged to believe that outer appearances and behaviors determine our value. Partners of sex addicts frequently believe that if they were only more (or in some cases less) attractive, sexy, intelligent, shapely, submissive, or better in bed, they could alter the addict's behavior. Their self esteem, which may already have been damaged, falls even lower as they become more and more involved in trying to fill the insatiable needs of the addict by changing themselves.

Society imparts a strong message to women that, if there is something wrong with her relationship, there is something wrong with her. The sex addict is usually only too happy to confirm this belief. In addition, many therapists, not understanding the dynamics of sexual addiction unknowingly reinforce this societal message. One woman sought help from two counselors, who told her to go home and satisfy her husband's sexual desires, and all her marital problems would disappear. Of course she failed, thereby proving to herself, one more time, that she was not good enough.

The partner is not only subjected to sexual put-downs, she is also frequently a victim of emotional and verbal abuse from the addict as well. Over time, she will begin to believe what the sex addict tells her about herself is true. Like the addict, she will harbor a secret belief nobody will love her for who she is, but for what she does. Unable to gain a sense of worth by being sexual enough for the addict, the partner can often be found taking care of not only the addict, but the kids, her family of origin, even her neighbors, in a search for worth that she can only experience in a recovery program and by sharing this healing process with other recovering partners.

Low self esteem is the natural outcome of being a partner of a sex addict. Like many of the characteristics yet to be discussed, it is a core recovery issue for partners of sex addicts.

However, low self-esteem doesn't always have to be present to be in a relationship with a sex addict. Some sex addicts will pick a partner with high self-esteem. When I first began counseling partners of sex addicts I was surprised by how healthy some partners were. They knew internally that they had nothing to do with their husband's sexual addiction. They knew they were attractive, sexually competent, and that, for him to get better, it was his responsibility. They had clear boundaries and little tolerance for relapse. These partners do exist, but rarely do they attend ongoing support groups for spouses of sex addicts. Consequently, the recovery community rarely believes they exist.

In most cases these partners, state very clearly that he gets better, or he leaves. This healthy partner doesn't fear being alone, taking financial responsibility for herself or her family.

Typically this is not the majority of partner's of sex addicts. Most reading this book will have to address self-esteem issues in their recovery groups or therapy. Before we leave this topic of self-esteem I want to provide statistics on what recovery can do, and is now statistically proven, to increase your self-esteem. We asked the following question about self-esteem after recovery.

In my recovery I feel my self-esteem is:

14%	High
23%	Low
23%	Low
14%	Very Low

Let's look at these numbers in recovery, compared to being in the relationship with the sex addict without recovery. I think it is clear by the chart below that focusing on your personal recovery can help your self-esteem.

In the relationship		In recovery	Difference
High	05%	14%	+9
Average	20%	49%	+29
Low	38%	23%	-15
Very Low	37%	14%	-23

Now you see why I love my job! I enjoy seeing partners of sex addicts regain their self-worth and begin to believe in themselves. Partners once again begin to listen to their intuition and behave in such a way that she gives dignity back to herself. For some partners it is difficult because it is the first time that they have ever felt the worth flow through their blood. Others are going back to the persons they once were before the residual of addiction infected their values. Either way, it is a great sight to see the confidence they have in themselves as they leave my office, with a great future ahead of them.

As the partner begins to get more value in herself, the addict has to agree with her value and change behaviors, or find someone else to devalue. When she understands this, she will begin to see positive changes in her life and relationships. Go for it!

9
Black and White Thinking

Living in an addictive system creates and perpetuates unhealthy patterns of thinking and feeling. One of these patterns is called all or nothing or, black and white, thinking. Most addicts and partners of addicts live, think, and feel in extremes. They understand feeling way up or way down, and can be uncomfortable just simply feeling okay. They understand good and bad, but have difficulty with the concept that every human being has both good and bad qualities. They believe they have to have it all, or they can have nothing. In a relationship with a sex addict, this is manifested in a number of ways.

One example of black and white thinking is that the partner of a sex addict sees the addict as either all good, or all bad. She can focus on his sexual acting-out as evidence that he is no good, thereby creating some sense of esteem for herself (at least, she's not doing those terrible things.) This works as long as the sex addict is acting-out. When he does something kind or loving, however, she will feel confused. She will switch to thinking she was all wrong about him, and that he is, indeed, all good. Or, he will deny that he is acting-out, and, out of a need to believe in his goodness, she will discount evidence to the contrary, no matter how obvious it is. Always focused on whether he is good or bad, she will be unable to focus on herself and make decisions about her own behavior, or value herself independently of who the addict is today.

Another example of an extremes belief system is reflected in the partner who believes *she* is either all good or all bad. At any given moment, her behavior will reflect whether she believes she is good (often exhibited as a holier-than-thou attitude, or grandiosity), or bad ("I'm worthless and deserve to be treated as such"). On the other hand, this partner can feel all bad on the inside and be compelled to project an image of being all good on the outside. She will frequently insist that her family members do the same thing, and be intolerant of behaviors in herself, or others, which disturb the surface image of a good family. She understands feeling perfect and feeling worthless, but has limited experience of the in-between. Anything less than perfect is worthless, in herself or in others. Because of this, she can either love herself or hate herself, and love others or hate others, but leaves herself no room for other emotions. It's an exhausting existence, an emotional roller coaster, a frightening ride through life.

In the area of behaviors, black and white thinking again produces extremes. Partner's of sex addict will decide one day to leave, and the next day to stay with, her addict. She will make promises to herself and threats to the addict about things she will, and will not, put up with, then not be able to follow through. She will alternate between elation, when things are going her way, and depression, when they are not.

For example, she will set boundaries with the addict about a particular sex act, and unrealistically expect that she will be able to maintain her new boundaries within the relationship. Having made the decision, she will feel good about herself until she meets with the addict's insistence that she participate as she always has.

Black and white thinking is a no win situation for the partner, leading to constant inconsistencies in feelings and behavior, and perpetuating the trap of the addictive system. When it comes to expressing feelings, this all or nothing phenomenon can result in one partner expressing all the feelings in the relationship, and the other, remaining shut down. Or, there may be certain feelings that are permissible for one member to express, but not the other. Generally in our society, women are allowed the expression of sadness, but not anger. Men are more frequently allowed to express anger, but not sadness.

In the relationship with the sex addicted partner, this can be taken to extremes. For example, Becky rarely had to express her own anger - she would just tell her sex addict husband what had upset her, and he would rage. Afraid of her own anger - much of which would be directed at him, and possibly destroy the relationship if it was expressed, Becky chose work addiction as a way to run from her feelings, and allowed her husband to express all the anger in their household.

In another example, Ellen could cry in her relation-ship, and in fact, cried about a lot of things, a lot of the time. This allowed her husband to focus on what he termed her emotional weaknesses and appear to be the one in control. He convinced her that she would be unable to cope in the world alone, and she stayed stuck in a relationship where his sexual acting-out put her at risk.

When we look at the partner of a sex addict, this all or nothing approach is evident. Some partners spend the majority of their time appearing inordinately, even unnaturally, calm, competent, and in control. Then, something will trigger an emotional outburst that seems out of proportions to the situation at hand.

Julie was a single mother, very capable at her job, who had been in a recovery program for several years. She was dealing with her daughter's pending summer visit to her father, and found herself in a family therapy session, terrified and unable to stop crying. This was a side of her Julie rarely allowed herself, much less others, to see. She was as surprised as the therapist at the intensity of her feelings, and was able to recognize that she had been sending her daughter to visit her sexually addicted ex-husband twice a year, for years, without ever acknowledging to herself the terror that it created within her.

Julie had dealt, to some extent, with her own childhood abuse, but had never really addressed the sexual abuse she experienced in that marriage. She could not acknowledge her feelings that would not have fit with her image of a woman *in control*. It was okay to express the feelings of her own inner child (it's okay for kids to cry), but it was unacceptable that an adult would cry uncontrollably.

Like Julie, many women have been cut off from their feelings for so long, that they are terrified of expressing them at all. They are afraid of being overwhelmed. The desire to control feelings is very strong, and long-suppressed feelings have a tendency to surface when we least expect, or desire, them. To the partner who has never allowed herself to express her feelings, even the tiniest hint of emotionality is automatically repressed. Her feelings don't just disappear though, and they will show up somewhere. This is the partner who is likely to have ulcers, or other stress-related disorders.

Contrast this with the partner whose job it is to express everyone's feelings. She has no idea which feelings are hers, and which ones belong to someone else. She just acts them all out. She is often labeled neurotic, and appears emotionally out of control much of the time. Her responses, in most situations, are out of proportion to the events that are occurring. People tell her that she overreacts, and may spend considerable effort trying to calm her down. She may be accused of just wanting attention, and may shame herself for her behavior, all the while not knowing herself why she reacts so strongly to things. She doesn't understand that the people around her are relying on her to express all their strong emotions for them. This can be particularly true of the addict she is married to, or involved with. He is avoiding his emotions by acting out his addiction. She is likely to be attracted to the "strong, silent" types, and with good reason. It keeps them feeling "strong and silent" and superior, while she just looks emotionally messy.

The end result of black and white thinking, as with other behaviors we are discussing, is an unmanageable life, either outwardly apparent, or internalized. With her thinking, feeling, or behavior out of control, the partner will find other things to control.

Partners who have black and white thinking (not all do) have to work on a few paradigm shifts. The first paradigm shift is the world is not the way she wants it to be. Her pain, fear, confusion, and other uncomfortable, undesirable realities are, indeed, a part of life. These undesirable realities affect her and she **cannot** control them all from affecting her or the ones she loves.

A second paradigm shift that is important for the partner who struggles with black and white thinking is the reality that all people are both good and bad. This includes her, her husband and her children. I know the world would be a greater place if all people were good, but the facts are, we are not. Her sex-addicted husband can be good and bad at the same time as much as she can be. When this can be accepted, the need for the safety that black and white thinking provides for her subsides. This can lead to a healthier life for her and those who she loves.

10
The Need to Control

The need to be in control is another core issue for partners of sex addicts. The evidence of the need to control can carry from person to person, but the underlying compulsion is the same: the people, places, and things in her outer world must be arranged in a specific way for her to feel a sense of identity, value, and safety.

In my clinical experience, control seems to be a common issue for partners of sex addicts. In our survey of partners of sex addicts, we asked partners of sex addicts about their controlling behavior.

In your relationship with a sex addict, have you participated in controlling behavior?

    91%   Yes
    09%   No

Control is a normal reaction to being in a relationship

with an addict of any kind. They feel if they do this, or that, the addict will change. Unfortunately, what happens, in reality, is that the partner does the changing.

I have often heard partners say "I don't even like who I have become" and they are often referring to their need to control. Although control does not apply to all partners of sex addicts, it does apply to many.

When someone grows up in a household where the adults are out of control because of addictions, emotional problems, or where abuse is present, she develops a strong desire to control the things that are available to her to control. It's just human nature: when you give up control, or have control taken from you in one area of your life, you will pick up the slack in another area.

Partners whose first sexual experience, often as a young child, was with an abuser, lose their natural right to develop a healthy sexuality. They lose sovereignty over their physical bodies. In response, they control what they can.

Many partners develop eating disorders. A compulsive over-eater might use food to control her body size, thereby keeping others at a safe distance. She may also eat as a way to soothe herself when she is hurt or upset. An anorexic or bulimic may not have been able to control what was done to her in the past, but she can control what goes into her body.

One adult bulimic realized that, after working with a man who made sexually suggestive comments to her on a regular basis, she would go home and binge. She was in a recovery program for the eating disorder, and was really hard on herself for what she considered a relapse, before she made the connection between feeling violated by this man's behavior and the need to binge. Once she began to acknowledge her feelings, and discover their origin in her childhood, she could nurture her fears in healthier ways, and was less likely to binge.

People-pleasing can be another form of control. Many partners of sex addicts learned at a young age to please people, in order to avoid further conflict, no matter what the cost was to themselves. Some learned to be perfect in appearance or behavior, possibly believing if they were only good enough, the conflict would stop. As an adult, this kind of people-pleasing can be expressed in a variety of behaviors. One partner was always up, dressed, and had her makeup on every morning, so that her husband would never see her looking less than perfect. She was afraid he would find someone else more attractive. Unfortunately her efforts did not keep him from having an affair, which nearly destroyed their marriage.

Many partners will give in to sex with their addict in order to attain such necessities as being allowed to eat or sleep. Some partners will wear clothes they are uncomfortable with in order to please their addict and for fear of being abandoned, or they believe it will keep him from acting-out.

The people-pleasing, however, does not just involve the sex addict. It can extend to other areas of the partner's life as well. She may feel compelled to put herself second to just about everyone else. Because her inner feelings are often out of control (whether she admits it to herself or not), and because her sex addict continues to act out his addiction no matter what she does to prevent it, she can go to great lengths to control her home or work environments. Some partners have "perfect" houses, "perfect" children, "perfect" hairstyles, makeup, and wardrobes. Others are compulsive on the job and have a strong need to be the best at whatever they do.

At the other extreme is Karla, who described herself

as a "reverse perfectionist." She knew her house could never be perfect, so she made sure it was just the opposite, and rarely cleaned it. As she grew in her recovery, she recognized another important factor. If her house was messy, and there were a lot of things cluttering the floor, she believed that an abuser would be less likely to come into her room at night. Karla, as an incest survivor, found a creative way to control her environment and protect herself. Instead of being upset with herself because she couldn't seem to keep her house clean, Karla began to see that her behavior really made perfect sense to her and, in fact, showed a remarkable ability to survive a really tough situation.

Karla's story illustrates an important point. Many of the symptoms and characteristics, evidenced by partners of sex addicts, are merely coping strategies they developed as children, which have helped them to survive threatening situations. When seen as such, these actions feel much less shaming. What is important for each partner to recognize is that these behaviors are no longer helping her, but are in fact creating more pain and chaos in her life. Many do reach the point where they recognize that, what they have been doing is no longer working, yet they still feel helpless to stop it. This can be an emotional "bottom" that causes her to reach out for help, and she can begin to recover from the effects of being a partner of a sex addict.

Not all partners face the need to control because of abuse or bad families. As we have discussed, not all partners of sex addicts are controlling or co-dependent. The partner who is fortunate to grow up in a healthy family still runs the risk of picking up controlling behavior because now she is living in an unhealthy relationship.

The sex addict who tries to make most issues about you, and it is regularly you who is the problem, also demands some system of defence from you as his partner. Control can sneak its way in. I encourage you to examine the issue of control in your marriage, relationships, and parenting. Control is an illusion. It does not exist in any form, except in your responses to the real world.

11
Boundaries

Boundaries in relationships are about knowing "where I end, and where you begin." A boundary defines how far you will allow someone to come into your space. Partners of sex addicts rarely have healthy, intact, boundaries. Many don't realize they have a right to boundaries at all, and have difficulty recognizing when they have violated someone else's boundaries. Their boundary systems may have been damaged in childhood, through abuse and the denial of reality that comes from dysfunctional families, or they may simply be damaged by being a partner of a sex addict. Whatever the case, their physical, emotional, intellectual, spiritual, and financial boundaries are sure to need repair.

The following list illustrates different types of boundary violations reported by the partners of sex addicts.

Physical Boundary Violations

☐   Somebody invading your "space"
☐   Being touched without being asked first
☐   Being told what you can, or cannot, wear
☐   Being restricted in how much makeup you wear
☐   Not being allowed to come and go at will
☐   Being pushed, shoved, slapped, bitten, kicked, hit, punched, or choked
☐   Being tickled without permission
☐   Being threatened with a weapon
☐   Being forced to stay awake
☐   Being raped

Emotional Boundary Violations

☐   Being told, "you shouldn't feel that way"
☐   Having your feelings ignored
☐   Being exposed to uncontrolled anger
☐   Being threatened with abandonment or forced to leave
☐   Being called names
☐   Having affection withheld
☐   Being told you are responsible for someone else's feelings (You made me angry, sad, embarrassed, etc..)
☐   Being exposed to constant whining or pouting
☐   Not being allowed to cry
☐   Being forced to stuff your feelings out of fear of violence

Spiritual Boundary Violations

☐   Being forced into the role of mother, or Higher Power, to the addict

- [ ] Having your relationship with God decided for you
- [ ] Having the addict act as your parent or Higher Power

Intellectual Boundary Violations

- [ ] Being told you are crazy
- [ ] Being told you are stupid
- [ ] Having your ability to reason things out for yourself discounted
- [ ] Not being allowed to go back to school or work
- [ ] Being told you will fail
- [ ] Being blamed for your children's failures
- [ ] Having your parenting abilities discounted
- [ ] Not being allowed to make everyday choices
- [ ] Having your speech or grammar constantly corrected
- [ ] Having words put in your mouth

Financial Boundary Violations

- [ ] Not being allowed to earn, or spend, your own money
- [ ] Paying for necessities when the addict spent all his money on porn or acting-out behaviors
- [ ] Allowing the addict to take money from you to support his habit
- [ ] Being forced to account for every cent you spend
- [ ] Allowing the addict's spending to interfere with your, or your children's, welfare or health

Sexual Boundaries

Sexual boundaries can be one of the hardest boundaries to identify and maintain for partners of sex addicts. Being around a sex addict just seems to make any sexual boundary they might have dissolve. Partners find themselves being sexual without conscious knowledge that they don't want to be. They become paralyzed by fear, and totally unable to protect themselves. Giving away their power is their automatic response to men, in general, and to sex addicts, in particular.

Partners find themselves, time and time again, in a powerless position. Each time they may strongly desire to set a boundary, they are unable to. In that moment, they feel like a child: frightened, alone, defenseless, unable to make appropriate decisions and act on them. Afterwards they blame themselves, not the sex addict, for the boundary violation.

In recovery, each situation that involves a sexual boundary violation, or any boundary violation, can become an opportunity for standing up and strengthening yourself.

Sexual Boundary Violations

☐   Not respecting your right to say no to sex
☐   Touching you in a sexual way without permission
☐   Making demeaning comments about women
☐   Treating you as a sex object
☐   Criticizing you sexually
☐   Withholding affection and sex
☐   Exposing you to pornography
☐   Insisting you wear sexual clothing that you are uncomfortable with
☐   Expressing interest in other women while with you
☐   Sexualizing affectionate touch from you
☐   Unsolicited comments about your body
☐   Unwanted staring from a man

- ☐ Demanding sex, or certain types of sexual acts
- ☐ Minimizing or ignoring your feelings about sex
- ☐ Having affairs outside an established relationship
- ☐ Exposing you to sexually transmitted diseases
- ☐ Sadistic sex
- ☐ Making sexual jokes
- ☐ Buying you clothing that you are uncomfortable with as a gift (This is really a gift for him.)
- ☐ Continually asking for a specific sexual behavior that he knows you are uncomfortable with
- ☐ Being physically forced or threatened with harm if you do not perform certain sex acts.

These lists are by no means complete. Boundary violations are the rule, not the exception, in a relationship with a sex addict. Don't be alarmed at how damaged your boundaries have become. You may have been in some denial about your situation for a long time. For now, just be aware that, with time and support, you can repair your damaged boundaries. (For more information on boundaries read *Partner's Recovery Guide,* where it goes into great detail about reestablishing your boundaries.)

12
Denial

Denial is a necessary survival mechanism, accessed in a variety of disease or trauma situations. As part of an overall grieving process, denial is one of the first defenses one may experience in an attempt to deal with a painful reality. Having a partner who is a sex addict is most certainly a painful reality.

In brief, the grieving process is as follows:

Shock	Feeling numb, almost beyond feelings
Denial	Not believing it: "It is too painful, so I'll just say it doesn't exist."
Anger	"I hate God, or them, for letting this happen"
Sorrow/ Depression	Feeling sad, or down, about the situation
Acceptance	Accepting the reality, and making healthy choices

Many aspects of this grieving process are discussed further in the *Partners Recovery Guide*. For now, we will focus on denial.

For partners of sex addicts, denial can be the hardest part of the grieving process. Partners of sex addicts deny that there is anything wrong with their spouses, their relationships, or their lives. Many look well put together on the outside, but are struggling hard to keep up the facade of having everything under control.

They are extremely good at denying the visible proof of sexual addiction: pornography, time, and money unaccounted for, and diseases they contracted from their husbands. One woman, when told by her gynecologist that she had a sexually transmitted disease, determined that she had contracted it from a toilet seat, and never even discussed it with her husband. She just knew there was no way he could have been exposed to it, even when her doctor told her it was highly probable. Only several years later, when her husband was confronted by a family member about the abuse of his niece, did the truth come out. This was the partner's denial, not the sex addict's.

Partners of sex addicts don't just deny what is going on outside, and inside, of them, but most are extremely out of touch with their feelings, and use a variety of compulsive behaviors to keep painful emotions out of their immediate consciousness. They may eat or sleep too little, too much, overspend, constantly keep busy, and compulsively clean things. Many of these women's lives might not look unmanageable on the outside, especially if they have been responsible for keeping a family going. If they ever stopped long enough to notice, their inner lives would be full of unacknowledged emotional pain.

Acknowledging reality can be a very painful thing that many partners want to avoid. Denial is the method they use to avoid feeling it. Have you ever done any of the following?

- ❏ Said, "He is Mr. Charming and Wonderful, so how could he have such a problem?"
- ❏ Only looked at the good he did, and never asked where he had been, or what he was doing.
- ❏ Internalized the problem, saying, "If he has a sex problem that means there is something wrong with me."
- ❏ Been too embarrassed to even think about him having a problem when you have such a happy family.
- ❏ Believed all men want sex a lot, and that's just the way they are.
- ❏ Said, "He was my first sex partner, and he is more experienced, so this sexual behavior must be normal."
- ❏ Having grown up sheltered, believed that this must be how everyone has sex
- ❏ Told yourself, "I married him, so now I am stuck. I made my bed, and now I have to lay in it."
- ❏ Said, "Well, at least he doesn't drink or smoke or beat me." (Minimizing his sexual acting-out.)
- ❏ Said, "Well, he just has a stronger sex drive than me"
- ❏ Rationalized that, "He is just being considerate not to bother me, so he masturbates late at night."
- ❏ Told yourself, "He deserves some time for himself. He works so hard you know."

These statements, and many like them, are prime examples of denial. Denial is powerful. Unfortunately, avoiding pain through denial prevents us from seeing the obvious. It keeps us from identifying the clues the addict may be leaving.

This denial is deadly, not only to the marriage, but to the entire family. If she never moves past denial, the partner can have some of the following serious consequences.

- ❑ It can keep the sex addict in the most isolated pain he can endure: the shaming of his sexual being.
- ❑ It can allow other members of the family to act out sexually addictive life-styles without ever being noticed by the parents.

It is necessary to struggle and move on through the grief process, and acknowledge these painful realities. As long as denial exists, reality does not.

If you are a partner of a sex addict, and denial has been helping you in your marriage, moving on will be a peeling away process. I find the quicker a partner is willing to take full responsibility for her own life, and for her family, the quicker she leaves the camp of denial.

Leaving denial is painful and can cost you friends, family relationships and even a marriage, along with your immediate financial stability. I would encourage you to write in your journal daily, feel your feelings, and experience the truth of his addiction, and the betrayal of your heart. This journal can serve as a reality check when you might want to go back to the comfort of "It's not really true," or "It's not that bad."

Have the courage to live in reality, no matter how hard it is. Remember you have a responsibility to yourself, and your family, to be real and not to pretend. You wouldn't want to teach your children that, would you?

Denial can keep everyone you love trapped in the chaos of the sexual addiction dynamic. Unfortunately, it is usually the partner of the sex addict to be the first to leave denial. The addict is drunk with fantasy and sexual obsession. The partner of the addict is usually the only hero in touch with reality enough to take the first step out of this insanity.

You will want the help of a support group, to help keep you out of denial, after the discovery of his sexual addiction. At first, you may be the only one in reality, but as you stand fast in it, the reality will increase. This does not guarantee that he will come out of his denial. Unfortunately, this reality is often a ladies first-dance, but as you step out, the music can finally change.

13
Dependence vs. Independence

A question that clients frequently ask is "Am I co-dependent?" I hear this question often, and there is no single answer. Partners vary widely in experiences, from someone so dependent that others make most of their decisions, to the very independent type where she is her own person and makes her own choices.

The discussion of levels of co-dependency can be the topic of many support groups and on-line chats. I believe in our study of partners that it would be important to see what partners feel about this issue. The following questions were asked pertaining to co-dependency.

I feel as if I was co-dependent prior to my relationship to a sex addict.

63%   Yes
37%   No

I feel as if I was co-dependent during my relationship to a sex addict?

85%   Yes
15%   No

There is a significant jump of 22% in partners feeling that they are co-dependent, while in their relationship with a sex addict, as opposed to before they were in the relationship. The co-dependent woman is most attractive to a sex addict, especially if he is going to live life irresponsibly emotionally and spiritually immature. The sex addict is clever to partner himself with someone who is very responsible and will help manage his life so that he can act-out.

Increased feelings of co-dependency are really to be expected in this relationship. Partners also increase in compensating behaviors and/or beliefs to try to make the relationship work and keep the family together.

On the other hand some partners of sex addicts do have feelings of self-worth, have healthy boundaries and do not at all feel co-dependent. This partner, who is in the minority, may feel outnumbered and confused by the majority of her support group members. With the group's ability to accept others where they are and not pre-conclude that all partners are co-dependent, the group can maximize the strength of each individual. An independent type partner can really help, yet sometimes irritate, other partners that have feelings of "woe is me" or "I don't know what to do," which often means, "I don't want to be responsible for myself," and make better choices. This frequently happens in groups, but if both are willing to stay long enough they can learn from each other.

As we have discussed, dependency is a common

theme in the lives of partners of sex addicts; yet there appears to be two extremes in their discussion of dependency. One type of dependency often observed in the lives of partners is called co-dependency or, in some cases, total dependency. The co-dependent woman chose to be in a dependent relationship with her sex addict.

Co-dependency will unmask itself in a partner's need to have her sex addict make her feel good about herself. She often has low self-esteem, and can't really believe she is worth being loved and enjoyed as the person she is. When a sex addict charms her in the beginning stages of a relationship, and tells her how special, beautiful, and good in bed she is, she feels loved and important, for perhaps the first time in her life. She will stay in the roughest of relationships, put up with, and even perform, sexual acts she doesn't feel comfortable with, rather than face the loneliness and sense of worthlessness that she experiences when she has nobody to love her.

This dependency will also be evident in her social life. Many partners of sex addicts who are in this co-dependent, or total dependency type, of relationship, will have limited or even nonexistent relationships outside of the one they share with the sex addict. This social dependency means that she finds herself relating only to the friends of the sex addict or his family. It never occurs to her in this dependence stage that she really wants and needs her own friends. Some partners of sex addicts try to develop friendships, but give them up the moment the sex addict disapproves or for fear he may sexually act out with her friends.

Social dependency can lead to the most frightening feelings of isolation. Some partners have lost close friends after these friends have observed his behavior, or if they have been sexually harassed by him.

Partners

Life can become a living nightmare for the dependent partner of a sex addict. She feels even greater pressure, though, if her dependency includes financial dependency. This is an utterly powerless position for the partner of a sex addict. She may believe, "What can I do anyway? I don't work, and can't support myself, let alone my children." She may have exhausted all other financial resources, and be too ashamed to run back home to her family, or call an old friend, for fear of them saying, "I told you so."

One more part of total dependency is "dependency of thought." With this dependency the partner gives up her freedom to think, or believe in what is right or wrong, good or bad. This dependency is the hardest to break away from. It manifests itself in fear of what her sex addict will do if she begins taking care of her own needs, and her listening to her internal feelings about what is good for herself. She becomes afraid he will leave her, or have an affair. The list of what he might do goes on and on. If the partner of a sex addict is to gain any sanity, she must first overcome her dependency of thought.

No discussion of dependency is complete without sexual dependency. Sexual dependency occurs when the partner allows her sexuality and sexual needs to be defined by her sex addict. Partners of sex addicts often allow their sexuality to be suppressed to the point of nonexistence, in an attempt to meet the standards of performance the sex addict defines as "good enough" for him.

The surrender of her own sexuality can leave her without knowing how often she really wants to have sex. Sexual dependency can also blind her thoughts as to whether or not she wants to be the pursued or the pursuer in the relationship. When she hears from him, "You've just lived such a sheltered life," she may begin to question herself, and then avoid responsibility for her own sexual boundaries. One partner's stated goal when she started recovery was to discover and define her own sexuality. She was 36 years old.

The eventual disintegration of their sexual boundaries, combined with a dependent relationship, causes many partners of sex addicts to perform sexual acts that they are not comfortable with, and later often feel shame about. This also comes about due to a lack of a sense of their own sexuality, and becomes more open to being talked into these uncomfortable sexual experiences.

The sex addict can then use this guilt and shame later to force her to continue a certain sexual behavior or to lure her into even more bizarre sexual acts. Giving up her sexuality often causes this partner to feel anger and distance toward the sex addict, causing a diminishing desire to even have a sexual relationship with the sex addict. When a partner feels exploited, it is usually an undeniable cue that she has surrendered her individual sexuality in her relationship with the sex addict.

In support groups, where these partners are dealing with problems of self-esteem, social, sexual and mental dependency, there may be another partner in the room, who is sickened at the thought of being dependent on anyone, especially the sex addict with whom they have a current relationship.

These partners appear to have great self-esteem. They look good, have professional careers, but have often only reached the second developmental stage of dependency which is independence. They may look great on the outside, but they are emotionally insecure. They need to be loved, but are not able to admit to their needs. Like many adolescents, they can't ask for a hug, even though they may need one desperately.

The independent partner often experiences several internal struggles. When it comes to self-esteem, she looks good; often, she looks perfect. She is the one with color coordinated everything, including accessories. She desperately attempts to control how others perceive her. She often exhibits very controlled emotions. She may have the reputation of being cool, calm, and collected. But this surface appearance is only one side of the coin. The side she keeps hidden is her insecure side. She can't trust others with real feelings of pain, self-disappointment, inadequacy, and nervousness. She has to look good, and this need creates a serious dilemma for her.

The independent partner creates walls of mistrust to cover her low self-esteem. She doubts others' thoughts, and motives toward her. She is often ashamed, but will cover her shame with logic or aggression in her relationships.

Because she can't trust others, this partner finds she must be independent, since she believes she is the only person she can trust. Yet, she knows that sometimes she can't even trust herself, because she continues to pick men who can see her genuinely low self-esteem, and exploit her. It's a scary scenario for her when she can't trust herself, yet can't trust others either. This lack of trust in others is a symptom of independency and a need for control.

The social side of the independent partner also has an internal struggle. This partner desperately needs to look good. Her sex addict may have some very positive qualities such as being extremely handsome or well built. He may have money, or look like he has money. He may be the "great catch" at the office, or some other social group.

Once she establishes a relationship with her sex addict, her need to control how he sees her becomes very evident. She often will change entire groups of friends when she meets her new sex addict's friends as well.

The "everything is wonderful" drama commonly characterizes the behavior of this woman. After all, how could somebody as smart as she is pick anyone less than wonderful? When the sex addict she chose begins to look less desirable, she will be able to break off the relationship quickly. This would be a positive sign, except for the fact that, a few days or weeks later, she will find another sex addict who is wonderful for her self-esteem and her social needs. The drama continues, but with a different group to impress, control, and hope for acceptance from.

The thought dependency dilemma for the independent partner is similar to her problem with self-esteem. Again, this partner may be known as a good thinker, even considered clear headed. But again, she feels she can't trust the insights of others.

Her thought "independence" can be very confusing as she finds herself in denial about who she really is: just another human being, with weaknesses and feelings, who is not in control of her life. Her need to control her mate, her children, or her work becomes an obsession; she rationalizes that she must use more time and energy, to work harder and longer, so she can keep things in control better. Her thought control increases her frustration, because she believes her only trustworthy source of insight is herself even though her own thinking lands her in the same place, time after time. It is a sweet victory for this partner when she can finally begin to trust others to think along with her about herself and her choices.

Sexually, this partner may also appear to have an independent disposition. The old, "get them before thy get you," theme is often a part of her sexual dynamic. Most sex addicts love and enjoy this type of sexual behavior. Her conduct gives her the illusion that she is choosing to be sexual because she can initiate sex and satisfy her "experienced" sexual partners. It may even be the foundation upon which her sexuality is built. But there is a price to pay for this illusion.

This partner must often be independent in order to be sexual. She associates independency with being sexually attractive to her partner when seducing him. But her attitude of wanting sex, "when I want it, the way I want it," is just another form of control. She needs to control her sexual activity, because feeling out of control frightens her. She may have a history of sexual abuse or rape, or she may just not be able to trust another person with her emotional and spiritual self. Like the addict, she uses sex to create emotional and spiritual distance, the safety of detachment.

This form of sexual behavior may, for a while, be physically satisfying. Eventually she longs for intimacy in sex, although she can't trust enough to be emotionally intimate, for fear of losing control. She doesn't recognize that truly intimate behavior is more than just physical trust. Her boundaries may become rigid and controlling, and she may be unable to enjoy the sexual encounter she initiates. In extreme cases she may find herself, not there, during sexual experiences with her sexual partner.

This dependency/independency tension is part of the black and white thinking of partners of sex addicts. These partners need to understand the normal stages of dependency, so they can see where they are individuals and grow into healthier people, who don't violate their beliefs and themselves, or feel the need to violate others by the relationship choices they make.

Dependency

Everyone is born into this world in a state of total dependency. Babies are unable to feed or bathe themselves and are totally dependent upon, and vulnerable to, the whims of those to whom they were born. During this stage, they learn how to manipulate their environment to meet their inner needs for love, affection warmth, food, and entertainment. This dependency on family or other caretakers continues. As the child grows, he or she remains dependent for food, clothes, and money for other aspects of everyday life.

Unfortunately, there are those who never leave this dependency stage. These children may leave home, but recreate the family of origin with friends, lovers, or mates. A person who remains in this stage will still rely on the ability to manipulate those around him or her, to meet their needs for self-esteem, acceptance, to feel beautiful, sexual and intelligent. This endless list of needs becomes the responsibility of those they place in their role of parents (i.e. lover, friend, husband, boss).

The demand that these needs be met is often presented with an attitude of entitlement, such as you would expect from a child. This person really believes, "You're supposed to do this for me" or, "You're responsible to meet this need in my life." They will often have great difficulty understanding why other people don't put their needs first, and they will use techniques like guilt, shaming, blaming, pouting, and isolation or tantrums to get their way.

If you are reading this and are thinking, 'I don't do this" ask yourself, "Am I in touch with my real needs, and do I have to ask permission from someone to get these needs met?" If you immediately think of someone from whom you get permission, you are probably stuck in the dependency stage with that person.

When you realize you may be in a dependency relationship with a sex addict or other person, you may have feelings of anger that you can't think your own thoughts, or meet your own needs, or create your own reality.

This reality often hits home when a partner is thinking about a separation or divorce. She may tell herself, "I can't leave him," and then list the multiple ways in which she has become totally dependent upon him. She comes to the same conclusion many children often do: "I can't run away." These feelings of being a child in a relationship are painful, but must be faced before moving into a healthier life-style.

Ironically, the dependency stage does have its "payoffs." The dependent partner always has someone to blame for the fact that her life is empty, devoid of intimacy, or just plain miserable. This stage allows her to blame her sex addict for not taking care of her needs. It also gives her permission never to be responsible for her own needs, or responsible for her own behavior. "If he would just... then it would be better for me," she tells herself. This lack of insight into her own feelings, needs or even self-limiting behavior, is symptomatic of a partner in the dependency stage.

The avoidance of any personal responsibility must be examined by the partner of a sex addict, either in a support group or in therapy, if she is ever going to enjoy the freedom of being a responsible adult who is able to choose healthy relationships.

Independency

Healthy children continue to grow until they reach

the stage of adolescence. This stage is full of rapid changes in their bodies, in their ability to think, and in their desire for sexual relationships. In this stage, childlike behavior becomes subject to thoughts about abstract things, such as right and wrong. If a child knows when "that's not fair," it is a good indication that he or she is moving toward independence.

Moving further away from mother and father is a good and natural developmental stage that everyone goes through. Adolescents learn that they can meet some of their own needs, especially when they start making their own money. They want to be treated like adults, though the small amount of money they earn could barely sustain much of a life-style.

What does this have to do with partners of sex addicts? Many partners get stuck in this independent stage of development. They buy, hook, line, and sinker, our cultural belief that to be totally independent from others, is good. They also buy into the belief that, in and of themselves, they should be able to handle all of life's situations, dilemmas, and crises in a calm, cool, and collected manner. Basically, this partner is stuck in the belief that she must be perfect, look perfect, and act perfect in all aspects of life. She denies a genuine human need to ask for help, just as a teenager might not admit to needing help from an adult.

This partner may use her sex addict for companionship, a false sense of intimacy (for neither the sex addict nor an independent partner can allow themselves to be out of control or vulnerable), or just for sex. She is certainly troubled by loneliness, and may even fight depression and suicidal thoughts.

Independence has a great price tag for a partner of a sex addict. She is not allowed to ask for real advice because of her basic mistrust of others and her environment. This can be costly when she realizes that she doesn't even trust herself or her own judgements, for fear of being wrong.

Fear is the basic motivation behind an independent partner of a sex addict. It is what fuels her need for control of herself, her addict, her relatives, her children, and how others perceive her on a daily basis. This fear affects all of her relationships, especially her marriage. She may appear loving and close, but inside, at her core, she cannot be touched. She is emotionally distant from her mate, even though she may be very sexually active.

She will usually have her own checking account, credit card, and car, and be totally self sufficient. While this may seem healthy, it allows her to pick sex addicts who need her to take care of them emotionally, and, often, financially. She slowly becomes the mother in the relationship. At this stage, she begins to question why she is in this relationship, and often may kick him out of the apartment or house she is paying for.

This partner usually looks "perfect," so others may think of her as somehow better than everyone else, and unapproachable. She would probably not admit that her need to be superior is motivated by fear of being inadequate or unloved.

This partner's apparent strong self-esteem is usually only on the surface, and often is very fragile. I find it amazing how some of the most beautiful women feel unattractive, and have a great need to feel accepted, even though they deny this need for acceptance and love.

This independent woman may feel good about herself, because she can physically and emotionally get rid of the sex addict to which she is attracted. She rarely thinks about how she is repeatedly attracted to a sex addict. She loses her boundaries in her next relationship, and is off and running again: running from the loneliness, the need to be genuinely loved for who she really is, the need for her fears to be accepted without criticism, and the need to move into the last stage of development, which is interdependency.

Wherever you may be in your journey in your relationship, I encourage you to evaluate your current status of dependency, independency, or interdependency. This can help you start a personal growth path toward the next stage. You may need the help of a support person or professional counselor.

Interdependence

This is the last stage of development where people can fully take care of themselves, including financially. They don't need anything from their "parents" but rather choose to simply be in a relationship. For the partner of a sex addict, this is where both persons in the relationship are adults and chose to be in the relationship with each other.

Interdependence is for those that have individually looked at their life and addressed their major issues. They don't stay in the relationship because they are dependent, but rather, because they choose their mate. Both partners are able to be spiritual, emotional, and sexual adults. Both partners can be emotionally safe and available for each other throughout their life.

You can only do your part in an interdependent relationship. Your spouse must also do his. He must address intelligently his sexual addiction and other issues. As an addict he will be emotionally and spiritually limited. If you both do your own work you can enjoy an interdependent relationship where you both choose to be connected to each other for a lifetime.

14
Depression

The fact that a partner can experience depression as a result of being in a relationship with a sex addict has been theorized, but not proven - until now. In our survey of partners of sex addicts, I asked partners about depression.

In the clinical field of sexual addiction, authors, researchers, and clinicians bantered the notion of the presence of depression in the lives of partners. Was the depression symptom we were seeing there prior to the relationship, or caused by the relationship? Let's look at some responses from partners first.

I feel that, prior to my relationship with the sex addict, I struggled with depression.

     39%   Yes
     61%   No

I feel that, during my relationship with the sex addict, I struggled with depression.

82%   Yes
18%   No

I was truly surprised to see depression increase 43% while these respondents were in a relationship with a sex addict.

If you are in this majority, you probably have suffered some degree of depression. It is a normal reaction to being in a relationship with a sex addict.

When you marry, you are to form an interdependence. A sex addict for the most part is incapable of this emotional mature relationship and when your soul is not being nurtured emotionally or spiritually depression can easily occur. In a relationship with a sex addict, it is often all about him, his needs, his sex, and his looks. This is emotional adolescence, not emotional adulthood. I have had many partners tell me how alone they felt in this relationship. Some who have husbands who are also sexually anorexic have a feeling that they are simply roommates with their addict.

A way to explain where this feeling may come from is to imagine a sponge inside of your soul. This sponge needs watering regularly to stay healthy. When the addict ignores your soul, your sponge gets dryer and dryer leaving you fighting symptoms of depression.

I can hear my colleagues saying, "so what?" These partners may feel that they are depressed, but do they fit criteria for clinical depression?

I wrote out the basic criteria for clinical depression in an easy to understand manner for our survey of 85 partners of sex addicts. These partners responded to this criteria for the period during their relationship, as well as how they were currently experiencing these symptoms. First lets look at their responses during their relationship with a sex addict.

74%	Poor appetite or overeating
78%	Unable to sleep or oversleeping
82%	Low energy or fatigue
71%	Feelings of restlessness or being slowed down
69%	Poor concentration or difficulty making decisions
78%	Feelings of hopelessness
33%	Suicidal thoughts
82%	Depressed mood
62%	Diminished interest or pleasure in most activities

In the clinical world you would only need five yes answers to be viewed as clinically depressed and in need of therapy or medical treatment. The numbers in the above chart reinforced that not only do the majority of the partners feel depressed, they actually are clinically depressed. This research assists clinicians in helping partners of sex addicts.

I now am much more aware to ask partners about depression, if it does exist evaluate clinical approaches, as well as medical options, if necessary. Not only are most partners often not getting their internal sponge moistened with consistent love (not just when they want sex) but many have felt real anger or rage over their sex addict's behaviors toward them. Their physical body can only store so much emotional pain before the energy to suppress and control the rage within steals from their energy to enjoy life.

Many of you know I am very much an optimist, and I wouldn't just leave you here on the subject of depression without offering hope. We asked these very same partners (of which 82% stated being in active recovery) about these same depression symptoms in their present recovery.

During my present recovery I experienced:

- 47% Poor appetite or overeating
- 45% Not able to sleep or oversleeping
- 49% Low energy or fatigue
- 39% Feelings of restlessness or being slowed down
- 40% Poor concentration or difficulty making decisions
- 44% Feelings of hopelessness
- 18% Suicidal thoughts
- 48% Depressed mood
- 28% Diminished interest or pleasure in most activities.

I think it is very obvious from these responses that partners in recovery reduce their symptoms of depression. Again, the residual of living with a sex addict can be depression. If you have a normal response to sex addiction, you might be experiencing symptoms of depression and you may want to consider individual therapy or talk to your doctor about medical treatment.

As a whole, this research confirms that these partners have significantly decreased their depression symptoms in recovery. Let's look at these numbers now, side-by-side this time.

	In Relationship	Now	Difference
Poor appetite or overeating	74%	47%	-27
Unable to sleep or oversleeping	78%	45%	-33
Low energy or fatigue	82%	49%	-34
Feelings of restlessness/slowed down	71%	39%	-31
Poor concentration/ difficulty making decisions	69%	40%	-29
Feelings of hopelessness	78%	44%	-34
Suicidal thoughts	33%	18%	-15
Depressed mood	82%	48%	-34
Diminished interest or pleasure in most activities	62%	28%	-34

Although depression appears to be a normal reaction to being in a relationship with a sex addict, your personal recovery can help put those depression symptoms back where they belong. For some partners recovery would include anger work and for others it would include individual therapy where past and present issues would be addressed along with the attendance in local support groups. Some partners may need medical treatment and still others need all these resources. Whatever your needs may be, you are worth it to get better from the affects of this addiction.

15
Food

Research shows that this section on food issues seems to apply to about 50% of partners reading this book. **Not every partner has this issue with food** as a result of being in a relationship with a sex addict. A large number of partners who had these issues with food during the relationship with an addict, also had issues and coping patterns prior to the relationship.

In our study, we asked the question about using food as a reaction to being in a relationship with an addict. Let's look at the results of the 85 partners responding to this research and then discuss the results later.

I feel that, prior to my relationship with a sex addict, I struggled with eating disorders (not eating, binge eating, over eating).

    40%   Yes
    60%   No

I feel that during my relationship with a sex addict I struggled with an eating disorder.

62% Yes
38% No

As a result of living with a sex addict, we see a 22% increase of eating disorders. This is a significant increase for the partner of a sex addict. I think this is important because it may point to another reaction to a relationship with a sex addict. This could also be a part of how some partners express their symptoms of depression.

Regardless of the cause of this reaction I think it is important to validate that some partners have food issues that increase or begin by being in a relationship with a sex addict. Our research went further into this area of food issues for partners of sex addicts.

I feel that I have turned to food during my relationship with a sex addict.

59% Yes
41% No

To go even a step further, we asked about the partners specific type of eating disorder. There are three types of eating disorders we asked about:

1. Overeating
2. Bulimia (binge eating)
3. Anorexia (not eating)

Remember, that eating disorders did not apply to all

partners. Of those who did struggle with an eating disorder these are the disorders, they identified with (this only applied to those who identified eating disorders).

84%   Overeating
05%   Bulimia
11%   Anorexia

Of those partners who did struggle with an eating disorder, it is apparent that the overwhelming majority have overeating issues. This potential to turn to food was addressed further in our research with another question.

I feel I have gained weight due to coping with a relationship with a sex addict.

61%   Yes
39%   No

I am not going to leave you here destitute with what happens to some partners as a result of living with a sex addict. Let's continue to look at what partners have accomplished as a result of their recovery.

In my recovery I have addressed food issues.

46%   Yes
31%   No
23%   Does not apply to me

As we continue to walk through this section regarding food issues, we must acknowledge that some partners had food issues before their relationship with the addict. For others the relationship exacerbated these issues, and, for still others, there is a direct cause and affect to this issue.

I compassionately want to encourage those partners who struggle with the issue of food to address them in your recovery. You will have to take responsibility for your soul and body to heal completely from past issues and issues related to the sex addict. If you love yourself, this will be an important issue to address and will make a significant difference in your life.

16
Sexual Issues

Over the years, I have counseled a wide variety of sexual issues that were a part of the lives of the partners of sex addicts. Some of these sexual issues were a part of their lives prior to their relationship and others were there as a reaction to their relationship with an addict.

I will address these sexual issues that partners face in subcategories in this chapter beginning with the sexually healthy partner.

The Sexually Healthy Partner

The sexually healthy partner needs to be addressed in this sexual issues section. Not every partner in a relationship with a sex addict has sexual issues, or is a victim of sexual abuse. This needs to be said, loud and clear, to validate this minority group present in recovery groups and who often feels left out, or not heard.

This partner grew up sexually informed, made good sexual choices, wasn't sexually abused, and didn't participate in any of sexual behaviors that the addict may have requested. She doesn't have a core belief that she is bad, nor does she believe that her sexuality is bad. She can be sexually assertive and doesn't have difficulty talking about sexuality. This partner doesn't feel ashamed of her body, and, in no way, does she feel his sex addiction has anything to do with her. She believes that *he* has the problem, if he thinks she isn't enough.

If you are in this minority, I know you are feeling heard and appreciated, while the majority reading this book are thinking "no way, she doesn't exist." Although I have counseled with this healthy partner on occasion, let's go to our survey for some support. I asked partners in our study about their sexual boundaries during the addiction as well as after their recovery.

I feel like I had clear sexual boundaries with my addict during the addiction.

    37%   Yes
    63%   No

I feel like I have had clear sexual boundaries with my addict during recovery.

    66%   Yes
    34%   No

There is a percentage of partners who maintain their own sexuality, even in the course of a relationship with the sexual addict. Also, it is revealed that a partner in active recovery is likely to improve in the area of sexual boundaries.

The Sexually Scarred Woman

In the field of sexual addiction, there has been an unchallenged paradigm that most, if not all, partners are sexual abuse victims or, in some way, have been damaged sexually. As a researcher in the field of sexual trauma, I wanted to determine in this study to see if this paradigm was true. Past research on sexual abuse for women is generally placed at about 30 to 33%. I compared this research with partners in relationships with sex addicts, to see if they fall above or below this general percentile for sexual trauma. I asked the partners in the study about their history of sexual abuse.

I believe I was sexually abused.

> 40% Yes
> 60% No

Sexual abuse is an issue for less than half of the partners in relationships with sex addicts. Although this is above the average of 30 to 33% it hardly represents the majority of partners in recovery.

For those who have been sexually traumatized prior to the relationship, or during the relationship, your pain is very real and can affect many areas of your life. In this study, 41% of the partners reported that their first sexual encounter had a direct impact on their sexual behavior with the sex addict.

If you have been sexually abused, I strongly recommend you seek professional help. You are worth the healing that can take place in this area of your life.

Women Sexually Scarred by Addict

There are some sex addicts who try to have their partners participate in their sexually addictive behaviors. The addict may continue to chip away at his partner for years to try to get her to do this behavior "just one time." The behaviors can be anything. Some partners in our study stated they participated in threesomes, group sex, swapping, anal sex, sex with other men or women, sex with someone else, while their husband watched, phone sex, bondage-the list goes on. I have heard many partner's stories where they were scarred sexually during their relationship with a sex addict.

The addict may repeatedly rape his partner or he may sexually shame her by say things such as "You're no good. You're a bad lover." The sexual shame and abuse that can occur in this relationship cannot be communicated deeply enough here. We asked the partners in our study to respond to this issue.

In my relationship with the addict, I have participated in sexual behavior of which I am ashamed.

50%   Yes
50%   No

This pain is real, and so is the shame and sexual scarring for some partners in this relationship. To heal from this deep pain, it must be talked about and often worked through in therapy. If this is something you may have experienced, along with the partners in this study, share this with the other members in your support group, and seek professional help from someone who treats sexual trauma issues.

Sexual Diseases

Sexually transmitted diseases (STD's) is an issue for partners of sex addicts. Although some sex addicts are strictly masturbation addicts, some do stray outside of a monogamous relationship. When an addict goes outside the relationship, he is usually in the altered state of his sex addiction and is disconnected from sane thinking about sexual diseases. Even if he did use a condom, they are only 70 to 80% effective, depending on the studies you read. That still leaves you vulnerable to STD's. We asked the partners in our study about this issues.

In my relationship with my addict I contracted:

> 23%   1 STD
> 05%   2 STD's
> 72%   Not contracted any STD's

Even though almost two-thirds of the partners have not contracted any STD's, there are those that have contracted a wide variety of diseases. I have counseled partners that are now unable to have children because of the disease they contracted from their sexually addicted husband. This is a painful reality; and you can't rely on the addict to tell you the truth about your risk of sexually transmitted diseases. In our study, 70% of the partners had been tested for STD's. I strongly recommend, if you are a partner of a sex addict, that you be sexually responsible for yourself and talk to your doctor about getting a full battery of tests for STD's so that you can clearly ascertain your health status.

Sexual Anorexia

In a journal article I wrote called *Sexual Anorexia: A new paradigm for hyposexual disorder*, I surveyed three groups of people for sexual anorexia. The results of this survey are:

29% of male sex addicts are sexually anorexic
39% of female sex addicts are sexually anorexic
39% of partners are sexually anorexic

This study completed in 1998, helped the clinical community identify the prevalence of sexual anorexia in the three groups addressed. As a partner of a sex addict you need to be informed about sexual anorexia. The anorexia piece of sexual addiction can be more difficult for the addict and the partner to recover from.

In brief, sexual anorexia occurs when the addict actively is acting "in," within the relationship. He withholds spiritual intimacy, emotional intimacy, and sexual intimacy from his partner. He would much rather be with himself sexually than with her. If you characterize your relationship as feeling like you are "roommates" you may be living with a sexual anorexic.

In our study, we asked partners to fill in the criteria for sexual anorexia for their husbands during his addiction, as well as in recovery. We also asked them to identify these characteristics for themselves. In the study, the partners were not told that this was the criteria for sexual anorexia,

114

they simply answered the questions as listed.

Has your sex addict displayed these behaviors during your relationship while he was active in his addiction?

76%	Withholding love from you
72%	Withholding praise or appreciation from you
73%	Controlling by silence or anger
58%	Ongoing or ungrounded criticism of you causing isolation
62%	Withholding sex from you
86%	Unwillingness to discuss his feelings with you
81%	Staying so busy, he has no relational time for you
85%	Making issues/problems in the relationship about you instead of owning his own issues
52%	Controlling or shaming you with money issues

Here we can see that many partners feel that they are definitely living with a full blown sexual anorexic. The aloneness and neglect that goes with this part of the addiction is very painful. The good news is, that in recovery from sexual addiction, there was improvement in this area; still, close to one-third of the sex addicted husbands or men remain full-blown sexually anorexic. This leaves much work for the couple that needs to recover from sexual anorexia, as well as sexual addiction.

Has your addict displayed these behaviors during your relationship while in his recovery?

28%   Withholding love from you
32%   Withholding praise or appreciation from you
35%   Controlling by silence or anger
25%   Ongoing, or ungrounded, criticism of you
        causing isolation
33%   Withholding sex from you
39%   Unwillingness to discuss his feelings with
        you
42%   Staying so busy he has no relational time for
        you
39%   Making issues/problems in the relationship
        about you instead of owning his own issues
25%   Controlling, or shaming, you with money
        issues

As you can see, sexual addiction recovery can make dramatic changes in the addict. Yet, approximately one-third of the men are still struggling with sexual anorexia.

I asked the partners in our study this time to respond personally to the same criteria for sexual anorexia during his active addiction. Then I asked them to respond personally to the same criteria for sexual anorexia while in recovery.

Have you displayed these behaviors during your relationship while he was active in his addiction?

39%   Withholding love from him
39%   Withholding praise or appreciation from him
52%   Controlling by silence or anger
35%   Ongoing, or ungrounded, criticism of him,
        causing isolation
34%   Withholding sex from him
34%   Unwillingness to discuss your feelings with
        him

36%	Staying so busy you have no relational time for him
34%	Making issues/problems in the relationship about him, instead of owning your own issues
21%	Controlling or shaming you with money issues

Have you displayed these behaviors during your relationship during recovery?

18%	Withholding love from him
25%	Withholding praise or appreciation from him
25%	Controlling by silence or anger
20%	Ongoing or ungrounded criticism of him, causing isolation
25%	Withholding sex from him
18%	Unwillingness to discuss your feelings with him
18%	Staying so busy you have no relational time for him
22%	Making issues/problems in the relationship about him instead of owning your own issues
05%	Controlling or shaming him with money issues

I think there is enough evidence to support that, although some couples naturally clear up from symptoms of sexual anorexia, there are still approximately 30% of the addicts and 20% of the partners in recovery, that still struggle with sexual anorexia. These couples would do well to address this issue as soon as possible.

Sexual issues vary in range and intensity. As a couple evolves in recovery, they will often address these various sexual issues. Many of these issues, and more, are covered in the *Partners Recovery Guide*.

Sex can become a beautiful thing for the couple who does the work. If you both work on it together, sex can become beautiful again. I have counseled with many couples who, after addressing their sexual issues, state "This is the best sex of our lives." Often it is because both people in the relationship can now be intimate and sexual together, without guilt.

17
Defense Mechanisms

How is it that, in spite of all the issues involved in a relationship with a sex addict, that a partner can still survive in the sexually addictive relationship as it is? She probably uses a number of tools, or coping mechanisms, that she has developed over the years in order to survive. We'll discuss a few of them here.

Disassociation

Disassociation is a clinical term used to indicate a situation where someone is not fully connected with his or her current reality. It can be as simple as not being present where you are. You are physically present, of course, but mentally or emotionally you have distanced yourself from what's going on around you. Children frequently disassociate as they are being abused, thereby "losing" the memory of what happened to them. When memories of the events return, they are often seeing it as if on a movie screen.

Adults can disassociate too, and are often not even aware that they are doing it. If the events going on around a partner are too painful, she just goes numb. She may stay right where she is, but shut down emotionally. Life becomes a robot-like existence: she goes through the motions, but with little or no real involvement with those around her. She may look as if she is listening, but her mind is a million miles away. She may feel as if she is wrapped in cotton and can't really touch the people around her. She may literally have no idea what they have said to her.

Disassociation can last for a few moments, or for days, weeks, even years, at a time. For example, a woman might use disassociation in a sexual situation lasting minutes or hours. One woman, whom we'll call Maggie, reported that she regularly disassociated during sex, and would be angry later with her fiance for not having noticed that she wasn't really there. A woman may go through the motions of living for several days, taking care of daily tasks, but with no emotional involvement. Here is a description from one partner:

I was well into my recovery before I recognized when I was disassociating. I would be sitting with people, and they would be talking to me, and I would answer them, but all the time I was watching the whole scene as if from a distance, I could see myself walk and talk, and a part of my mind would be saying, "Can't they see that I'm not really here?" I would wonder to myself how I could function like that?

One way that disassociation can last for years is in a woman's inability to identify her own experience of current or past emotions. Have you ever gone blank when someone asked you what you are feeling about something now, or something from your past? It can be frustrating when you realize that you can't connect with your own emotions or with your inner-self in a positive, or even a negative emotional experience.

Disassociation affects the lives of partners in many ways. In the most general of ways, disassociation allows these partners to go through life, almost as if they live in some kind of fog. They can't seem to connect with what is real around them, and, left to themselves, sometimes can't even identify what is real. They may feel like a little, lost girl in a strange place, with big people all around, yet they can't find anyone who will nurture them, or help them connect, somewhere, to someone, or something. They may feel an ongoing ache of separation, yet perform as though they are okay, and nothing bad has ever happened. They tell themselves they will be okay, if they can just get connected somewhere, or get through a certain time period.

Disassociation also affects, and is affected by, the partner's relationship with the sex addict. Early in the relationship with the sex addict, she may be impressed with the way the sex addict expresses some of the more extreme emotions like passion, anger, rage, and apparently sincere tears of regret. These moments of intense expression touch something in a partner, allowing her to behave and feel alive for a few moments. She may even set up these sessions so that she can, in a very strange way, feel connected to herself.

She may never understand, when she is doing this, that the unrecovering sex addict can really only feel or express a handful of emotions; he often uses these emotions as tools to manipulate his partner into the bedroom, or to stay in the relationship longer than her instincts say she

121

should. The sex addict is an eternal opportunist, and can see dissociative behavior in his partner, and use it to his advantage. When she is disassociated, she is less likely to object to unwanted sexual advances.

Constant Busyness

Another defense mechanism that helps partners stay comfortable in an uncomfortable situation is constant busyness. Living with a sex addict cannot help but produce strong feelings, and staying constantly busy is a way to avoid those intense feelings. One partner worked 90 hours a week when she was married, so she wouldn't have to be at home and see what was going on in her marriage. Another partner reported that, when she was not at her full-time nursing job, she would stay up half the night cleaning, so she could avoid any sexual advances her husband might make. Yet another expressed how she spent hours each day cleaning her house because, as long as she was busy, she didn't have to think about where her husband was and what he was doing.

Peggy stayed overly involved in her children's lives, in an effort to avoid her spouse. Carla stayed busy with her job and the people she sponsored as a recovering alcoholic. She didn't want to see that her husband was acting out with many of the women in the Alcoholics Anonymous group. These partners all used compulsive busyness to avoid feeling their feelings, and to deny the reality of what was going on in their relationships.

Minimization

To minimize something is to make some occurrence or issue smaller than it is in reality. This is the reverse of making a mountain out of a molehill; it is making a molehill out of a mountain. The partner of a sex addict may use this defense mechanism to avoid her own reasoning or instincts about the sex addict's behavior. She may make statements like these:

- ❑ All men do this.
- ❑ It's only a phase.
- ❑ He needs more excitement than I can give.
- ❑ That's the way he grew up.
- ❑ The only way he knows I love him is to stick by him.
- ❑ What should it matter if I don't know everything he does?
- ❑ It could be worse; he could be an alcoholic or drug addict.
- ❑ He is such a good mate/husband/father, even though he does this.
- ❑ He doesn't beat me.
- ❑ He's a good provider.
- ❑ He's responsible in other areas.
- ❑ He pays the bills regularly.
- ❑ He goes to church.
- ❑ He helps other people.
- ❑ It really doesn't bother me.
- ❑ At least he always comes home to me.
- ❑ I'm the one he's married to.
- ❑ I'm the only one who has ever loved him; what will happen to him if I leave?

Statements of this type allow the partner of a sex addict to focus on at least some positive aspects of the sex addictive issues and dysfunction. This is like someone saying of the bomb dropped on Hiroshima, "At least it gave jobs to some people," without looking at the death and devastation it caused. Many partners do minimize in order to survive the devastation he caused in her life.

Why? The answer is probably different for each partner. Some partners have come up with these suggestions as to why they minimize the addict's behavior:

- ❑ It allows me to stay in the relationship if I don't look at what he is really doing.
- ❑ I don't have to feel my real feelings.
- ❑ I can avoid my feelings of rejection and abandonment.
- ❑ I don't have to deal with how ugly I feel when I'm not in a relationship.
- ❑ Even a sex addict relationship is better than no relationship at all, because that would mean nobody loves me.
- ❑ I don't have to take responsibility for my issues because I minimize these also.
- ❑ I don't have to question my own sexuality or sexual performance if I don't believe that he is getting more satisfaction from masturbation, pornography or other women.
- ❑ I don't have to shake up my financial and social world.
- ❑ If I looked at his issues, I would feel I'm to blame.
- ❑ My friends or family told me this would happen and I can't admit they were actually right.
- ❑ I can't raise the kids alone.
- ❑ I need him for manly tasks, and to be a father to our children.

❑   I would be too embarrassed if anyone really knew what he was doing.

❑   I can feel safe and loved if I don't believe the truth.

❑   I can't deal with people finding out I'm not perfect, or that our relationship isn't perfect.

Rationalization

Another deadly defense mechanism for partners of sex addicts is rationalization. This is the ability to make excuses, or come up with logical reasons for the sex addict's behavior or absence. This technique of not looking at the real situation, but creating a reasoning that colors the truth of the matter, is often the topic of recovery group meetings, and recognizing it is sometimes the most painful experience a partner will have in her support group or in therapy.

Most partners rationalized some of their own issues before they even entered into their first relationship with a sex addict. This makes it easy to transfer the rationalizing to their new situation. They rationalize, make excuses about the sex addict's behavior, or believe the excuses he gives them, even though they seem far fetched. Here are some examples from recovering partners.

❑   I know he's working late.

❑   There's nobody there to answer the phone after five but I know he's there.

❑   This big project is keeping him away.

❑   The case he is working on is way across town.

❑   He spends a lot of time shopping for the best price on all the items he buys.

❑   I'm looking through his wallet for the dry cleaning receipts or a certain credit card. I'm not prying.

- ❑ I'm meeting him later just to support him, not to check up on him.
- ❑ He has to use his credit cards for business and he charges out-of-town guests on his card locally all the time.
- ❑ He has to go to functions alone because it's strictly business.
- ❑ When he gets mad he always drives around for a couple of hours; that's just the way he handles his anger.
- ❑ I got this sexually transmitted disease from a toilet seat (even though the gynecologist tells you that's impossible).
- ❑ I have to perform oral/anal sex with him to make him happy.
- ❑ He is too religious to ever do such a thing.
- ❑ He just likes to help people. (But why are they always women?)
- ❑ I know she doesn't mean anything to him.
- ❑ These long distance charges are on our bill by mistake.
- ❑ I'll just bail him out this one time.
- ❑ The police are exaggerating his behavior.
- ❑ The baby-sitter must have called these telephone sex numbers when she was here.
- ❑ I don't know how these porn sites show up in our history file, it must be the kids.

Blame

Another defense mechanism that allows a partner to stay in denial is blame. She may either blame herself, or blame some outside person or situation for the addict's behavior.

The partner who is blaming herself, is likely to make such statements as, "I know he probably slept with her because I've gained so much weight the last few months," or, "If I'd only been a better wife/lover/mother/mate he wouldn't have done it." Others blame the other woman, it doesn't matter that the rival might really be several other women. Julie's first husband acted out with his sister's fourteen year old friend in their living room, while the family was asleep. When he told Julie about it, she confronted the girl he sexually abused, not her own husband, telling the girl never to do that again. This allowed her to deny that her husband had a problem, and allowed her to stay in the marriage.

Another woman, when told by her sex addicted school teacher husband that an eighteen year old cheerleader was carrying his baby, blamed the cheerleader for seducing him. Then, she took the girl to the abortion clinic, and sat there with her through the whole ordeal.

Some wives blame the boss or the job: "It's not fair of his boss to expect him to entertain those women when they're in town. It's not his fault." Whether a partner blames herself or outside circumstances, she is misplacing the blame. The addict alone is responsible for his actions and his choices. As long as she allows herself, or others, to shoulder the addict's responsibilities, she prevents him from feeling the pain that might motivate him to seek help.

It has been said that enabling is murder: if you enable someone to continue any addiction, you are helping him to kill himself. In sexual addiction, this couldn't be more true. Why then, do partners do it? Why do they deny, minimize, rationalize, become perfectionists, stay busy, blame everyone and everything, except hold the addict responsible for his illness? In a word, fear. Fear is such a great issue for partners that it deserves a section all its own.

Fear -- The Final Enemy

For the partner, fear is often a daily experience. She lives in fear of many things: fear of being alone, fear of being with someone, fear of intimacy (letting someone know who she really is), fear of being hurt, fear of other women, fear of her ability to make healthy decisions, fear of not being able to handle everything, fear of losing the illusion that everything is okay, fear of her past, fear of her future, and more. Let's look at some of these fears individually.

The fear of being alone is one of the biggest fears for many partners. Many of these women have not only justified some of the most bizarre behaviors or requests of the addict, but also their own tolerance of these behaviors, under the guise of, "Well, at least I'm not alone."

This fear is often repeated by women. They are afraid of being alone or even worse, being alone with their children. "How would I raise them alone?" a partner might ask. "I'd never make it on my own." These partners often fear being alone more than they fear being abused or misused sexually; even more than they fear the grim reality of their children being abused emotionally, physically, or even sexually.

For many partners, this fear of being alone is compounded greatly by shame. They may feel shame for being sexually abused, for participating in certain sexual acts with a current or past partner, or for getting pregnant before marriage. They fear what would happen if others found out, so they retreat into a life-style of isolation. They fear close relationships like they might fear a surgeon: the fear that people might cut through their masks and see the real pain they carry in themselves is so great that these partners stay away from others, and often convince themselves that they are not good enough to be in any decent type of relationship anyway.

Consequently, as these partners isolate themselves, they come to depend entirely upon the sex addict for self-esteem, acceptance and anything that even remotely reminds them of being loved. If he were to leave, her deepest fear of being alone would come true, so she does all she can to make sure that moment never happens. "I'd be so afraid not to be in this relationship, I can't even imagine it," one partner said in a meeting.

At the other end of the spectrum are partners who fear being involved in a relationship with a man at all. They fear once again finding a Prince Charming who, after being kissed, turns into a perverted little toad. They are often afraid of the "here we go again" syndrome. "He looks good but somehow I know it can't last," they may think. They fear being in a relationship with a man, because so often their past experiences have confirmed that all men want is sex. They might believe that all men will have affairs outside the relationship, and will eventually leave, so they tell them-selves, "I'll be alone anyway, so what's the use?" They would rather be without a relationship than take that risk again.

The fear of being unforgivable or unlovable also plagues partners. This fear manifests itself in deep shame. A partner of a sex addict might, in her bravest moment, acknowledge that what the sex addict does inside or outside the relationship is crazy beyond belief. She might, at times, have even wanted to take part in the sexual acts she has performed within this relationship. No matter what the reason, the partner believes that there is no way she can ever be accepted or loved by anyone else. She believes no one, including God, could forgive her for all the things she has experienced in her relationship with the sex addict. This compounds her need or desire to isolate herself from others.

The fear, that someone might discover the reality of her life, affects all of her relationships. Often when a partner is in love with a sex addict, her family and friends begin to ask questions about the relationship; she finds herself lying, or at least pretending, that nothing is wrong. Because she feels she must keep her shameful secret, the partner of a sex addict begins to isolate from her family and friends.

"What if they ever found out?" she thinks. "What if my husband or mate ever was mad at me, and told them what I did with him?" "What if they found his magazines in our house?" "What if he gets arrested for picking up a prostitute or for exposing himself?" "What if he hits on one of my friends?" Or even worse, "What if they find out about what I've been suspecting?" These fears grow and grow over time, until it becomes too difficult for the partner to reach out, even to the people who love her.

She may have other fears in the relationship as well. In addition to her fear of leaving the relationship, the partner might fear that her spouse might give her some type of sexually transmitted disease. She might fear that his pattern will never change, and that she is hopelessly doomed to stay in this relationship. She may fear that she will go crazy if she lives with this fear one more day.

Children are another area chock full of fear for the partner of a sex addict. She may fear that they will find his videos, magazines, or sex toys. She may also fear that the children will tell someone in school or in the neighborhood that their daddy likes other women.

130

The fears of partners of sex addicts might best be expressed in their own words. Here are some they have shared with us in support groups:

- [ ] I was afraid to stay, and I was afraid to leave.
- [ ] I was afraid I wasn't woman enough for him.
- [ ] I was afraid I could never please him sexually.
- [ ] I felt like there was something wrong with me.
- [ ] I was afraid I couldn't raise my kids by myself.
- [ ] I was afraid to let anyone know what was really going on in our lives.
- [ ] I was afraid people would tell me I had to stay.
- [ ] I was afraid people at church wouldn't understand.
- [ ] I was afraid nothing would ever change--that I was doomed, or that it would change, and he would leave.
- [ ] I was afraid to confront him.
- [ ] I was afraid, if I changed, nobody would like me, including myself.
- [ ] I was afraid it was my fault.
- [ ] I was afraid I could never find anyone else who would love me.
- [ ] I was afraid I was crazy, or would do something crazy.
- [ ] I was afraid I would kill him or myself.
- [ ] I was afraid he would get arrested.
- [ ] I was afraid he would give me some disease.
- [ ] I was afraid that he would lose his job.
- [ ] I was afraid that he would ask me to do that again.
- [ ] I was afraid I couldn't say no if he asked me to do that again.
- [ ] I was afraid I was a pervert.
- [ ] I was afraid he would tell others what I did.
- [ ] I was afraid my friends or family would find out.
- [ ] I was afraid he was gay.

❑ I was afraid that I wouldn't protect my kids.

❑ I was afraid everything he said was a lie, and that I would believe it.

❑ I was afraid every man was like this.

❑ I was afraid that people could see my shame about my life.

❑ I was afraid my children would tell.

❑ I was afraid I was only good for sex, and that my sex wasn't ever good enough.

❑ I was afraid of his anger.

❑ I was afraid when he came home drunk.

❑ I was afraid my kids would find his magazines.

❑ I was afraid my kids would grow up to be sex addicts.

❑ I am afraid I can't say no when someone I date wants sex.

❑ I am afraid to share my past with someone new I meet.

❑ I am afraid this guy will be like all the others; he'll look good at first, then I'll find out he has big problems.

❑ I am afraid that I'm emotionally or financially dependent on him.

❑ I am afraid I'll lose the only person who has ever said he loves me.

❑ I was afraid someone would find the pictures he took of me.

❑ I was afraid I'd never get better or be able to change.

❑ I was afraid that he was sleeping with our friends.

❑ I was always afraid. It seemed like all my decisions were based on one fear or another.

These fears can be overwhelming, and are often depressing. That is why it is so crucial that any partner reading this book realizes that she must reach out into the recovering community of other partners of sex addicts. She must create a supportive network for herself. Only then will she be able to talk about her fears and hurts, both past and present, and find other loving souls who will be able to listen and identify with her in a very deep and healing manner.

It may seem as if we have focused only on the negative aspects of being a partner of a sex addict. You may find yourself discouraged at this point, and wonder if there is any light at the end of the tunnel. Or, you might be saying to yourself, "I'm not that bad yet. I've never done some of the things others have talked about. I can do this on my own for awhile." You could be vacillating between these two extremes, and be overwhelmed and confused. Or, you might be well on your way to recovery, but experiencing a lack of confidence in yourself and your recovery program.

These defense mechanisms are often necessary to survive in a relationship with a sex addict. Remember you can not control him getting better but you can choose whether you get healthier. Recognizing any of your defense mechanisms may move you forward in your recovery and/or grief process. Life, in reality, can be painful at first, but, as they say in recovery groups, any single day sober is better than one drunk.

I encourage you to take some notes on this particular chapter and discuss this with your group members or therapist. You can be free of the need for these defenses, but it will take some time and the support of some other person or persons who understand.

18
Me Acting Out?

In support groups around the country this issue of acting out is discussed repeatedly. "What is my acting out?" is usually the way it starts in the group, and then the group responds, anything can be said at this point.

In the *Partner's Recovery Guide* we have a checklist which is used as a guide for partners so that they can check off whether they are staying clean from their acting-out behaviors. In our survey I asked several questions relating to the acting out of the partner of a sex addict.

First I want you to see how prevalent the behaviors are in our study. You can see by the below chart that only two behaviors on the list represent less than 50% of the partners in the study. These behaviors were present during the active days of his sex addiction.

85%   Checking up on him
78%   Being controlling
76%   Looking for more proof

68%	Spiritualizing or rationalizing staying together, when he is not recovering
68%	Feeling threatened or insecure around other women when you are with your addict.
58%	Not having sex or being hypersexual
66%	Reinforcing your fears of abandonment
65%	Trying to think about what they may be thinking about
64%	Not being able to separate when it makes sense
61%	Sarcasm
58%	Scoping out women he might be looking at
58%	Using his problem not to deal with your feelings
54%	Rages
52%	Shaming him
51%	Changing your boundaries with your partner
47%	Pretending you are in a perfect relationship
46%	Fantasizing about him acting out
36%	Spiritualizing the problem
18%	Hitting him

The partners in our study identified with many of the behaviors. We continued on this subject by asking these partners about the awareness of their acting-out behaviors. It appears that the majority of the partners understand when they act-out.

I understand what my acting out behaviors are.

87%	Yes
13%	No

Our survey asked these partners if they relapsed with their acting out behaviors. This would mean that the partner knew this was part of her recovery, but she does these behaviors anyway.

I have relapsed regularly into my acting out behaviors.

55%   Yes
45%   No

I am clean from what my acting-out behaviors are.

27%   For less than a week
25%   For one month
30%   For months
11%   For a year
11%   For several years (five year avg.)

As you can see from the above questions that roughly **half of the partners in our study are still acting-out**. This is a very important issue for the partner, as well as for the recovery groups for partners. If a partner is still acting-out, she will continue to propagate unhealthy beliefs toward herself and her recovery group. Likewise, it is important if half of the recovery group is still acting-out, because the group will waffle between unhealthy and healthy norms. The flavor of the group will be based upon whether the verbal people in the group fall into the acting-out portion, or the healthier portion, of the group.

I think it would be helpful for the partners in the group to clearly identify what their acting out behaviors are and how long they have been clean from those behaviors. The group members can then measure their feedback against their time actually clean. Who wants to listen repeatedly to a group member who chooses unhealthy patterns in her recovery? In a partners group this is an essential and healthy difference over some traditional Twelve Step groups.

One last question on this issue was whether consequences were set up for possible acting out behaviors. The partners had this response.

I have set consequences for what my acting out behaviors are.

  75%   No
  25%   Yes

You can see that the majority of partners have no consequences prearranged. As a clinician I know that, without consequences, the road to recovery is slow and long. To help you on your journey of recovery identify the behaviors that you might consider acting out (not what the sex addict considers). Once these behaviors are identified, be honest with a recovery person or group. Then set consequences for the behavior you have identified as unhealthy, and, lastly, keep your word. If you transgress follow through with your consequence, and it will make recovery so much quicker for you.

You deserve to heal from the affects of his sex addiction. Some of these affects are scars on your soul that are damaging your self esteem, your sexuality, and possibly causing depression. Part of the healing process is dealing with defense mechanism and shutting down behaviors that no longer work for you.

Remember, this healing process is for you. It is your responsibility to love yourself enough to want to heal. The addict <u>can't</u> heal you. He may, or may not, choose healing for himself. Regardless of his choice, you are responsible for the condition of your soul from here forward. I encourage you to do all you can do to become the person you are supposed to be: proud and confident. It may be a lot of work, but I can't think of anyone more worthy of it than you. I hope you agree.

19
Believing Behavior

A partner of a sex addict has often been deceived by her sex addict's addictive life-style. Sex addicts, by nature of the addiction, have over the years become masters of dishonesty. I can't tell you how many partners I have counseled that have been married many years, and honestly had no idea as to her sex addict's behavior. I remember one wife who found out about her husband's addictive behavior by breaking into her husband's safe and finding hundreds of women's underwear with names and dates, and a book full of phone numbers. All these years of marriage, she thought she was the only woman in his life.

I counseled with this woman years before the conception of the internet. Now I receive phone calls and e-mails regularly from partners, checking the history files on their computers and finding out the addict they are in a relationship with is into some pretty bizarre pornography. Ongoing deceit is exactly what a partner of a sex addict does not deserve to have happen over and over again.

One thing, that I have learned over the years of counseling addicts, is that they are the single most motivated people in the world. The greatest part about their motivation is that it is all internal motivation. Think about your sex addicted partner for a moment. If your addict wanted to develop a hobby or get involved in a sport or social activity, wouldn't he go all out to do this? If he wanted to learn how to fish or golf, he would probably buy the best equipment money could buy. He would read every book and go on the internet to related topics. He would even meet the local or national experts in that field so he could maximize this activity. Almost every woman married to an addict can identify with this aspect of their addicted spouse. Unless they are clinically depressed, they generally have this quality about them.

When an addict comes into my office, I know they already have all the skills I need for them to get better. They know how to meet new people, they know how to make phone calls to people they don't know, and they know how to read; even better, they know how to stay 100% focussed to get something done when they want to. They know how to create time to be somewhere if they want to. Every time I tell an addict this, they always laugh because all (and I do mean all) their excuses not to give 100% in their recovery is totally taken away.

When I ask an addict to start recovery by doing the basics which we call the Five Commandments of early recovery I know they can stay focussed to do it. The Five Commandments are very simple, but, when applied to the addiction, can put the addiction into remission. They are all behaviors that the addict does, not intends or promises to do. When addicts do these Five Commandments during the first 100 Days of recovery you can expect progress. The

Five Commandments are simple:

1. **Pray**: in the morning asking God to keep you clean today.
2. **Read**: literature related to sexual addiction recovery daily.
3. **Groups**: attend a Twelve Step or Freedom Group as much as possible.
4. **Call**: someone in the group daily to report your recovery status.
5. **Pray**: again thanking God for a day of sobriety.

These five steps may sound simple enough to you because, honestly, they are easy to do. If your addict only wants to do 1, 2 and 5, then he is not ready for recovery. Attending a group and making calls are truly the hallmarks of someone who wants to get better. Only those who want to get better (internally motivated) get better. Those that want to do it their own way are simply lying to themselves and their partner. Remember if you believe a lie instead of <u>believing</u> behavior <u>you are actively choosing denial</u>. That would not only be him lying to you, that would be you lying to yourself.

Believing his behavior is the only way for a partner to stay sane. If he doesn't attend groups or make recovery efforts, he doesn't want recovery, and you need to make hard choices for yourself and your family.

Also, in this same stream of thought, if you keep hearing that he "has to" do all these things instead of an attitude of "I get to" recover, then be concerned. Those who realize they are sick, and that they can get better, are generally so grateful that there is a name for what they have: sexual addiction, and that there is help for them. Look for creativity in your sex-addicted spouse's recovery. He will begin to create time for meetings, phone calls, and reading recovery material; you will begin to see him do more than just the minimum. Remember, always believe behavior.

While we are discussing believing behavior, we also need to talk about trust. In early recovery there may or may not be relapses with his behavior. How will you know if this happens? Some partners just believe that they will be able to tell when he acts out. Although that may work for some, I caution against this, in general, because of the nature of this disease, and the disposition of the partners wanting it to be all better.

Sex addicts lie about sex just like alcoholics and drug addicts lie about their drug of choice. Unlike other addictions, you may not see a trace of their acting out for years, and, in most cases, he has proved beyond a shadow of a doubt that he can withhold information from you and lie about his sexuality. So just trusting your intuition can be limited.

We include the following technique in our office as an ongoing part of treatment for sex addicts wanting to stay clean. What I am about to share, may sound drastic at first, and isn't needed in every case; however, I think it is important enough to address here. I also highly recommend a phone consult with myself or another therapist before you bring this to your addicts attention.

In our office a very credible polygrapher administers a polygraph test to the addict to determine 1) that he has been honest with the past, 2) to demonstrate ongoing sobriety at three, six, and twelve months.

Initially, the addict is stunned by this process, but as he realizes that this is the absolute shortest way to rebuild trust with himself and his partner, he begins to see the logic in having a report card for his recovery. If he is willing to do this ongoing in the first year, or longer if needed, you are in the best possible situation for recovery. I can't tell you how lives have been changed for the better, because partners feel they can once again trust their spouse. In my office we call it Report Card Day. I have men who fly from all over the country to take their test in my office, and have me call their wives to verify that he is still clean.

If your addict is unwilling to take a polygraph, you can often bet there is more to the story than he is telling you. It is reasonable for you to evaluate his level of honesty in this area of sexuality.

We have used polygraphs for years in treating sexual addicts. I think that is one of the reasons well over 80% of the men attending our Three Day Intensives stayed clean ongoing from the day they leave our office.

Now I must give a legitimate caution about polygraph operators. In some states they are not licensed or regulated by the state; I have had people who used a polygrapher outside of my office and were given a false read. Before you use a polygrapher in your area, I highly recommend that you call a few criminal attorney offices and see who they use. I can only stand behind the ones I use in my office. If you get references for a polygrapher, this can be a great way to believe behavior.

So far, we have discussed how to believe the recovering addict by looking at his behavior. You need to apply this also to your own recovery. What are you actively doing to heal from the affects of living with a sex addict? If all you are doing is looking at him, complaining, checking up on him and staying mad, you are not in recovery; you would still be considered acting-out.

You can also look at the Five Commandments, as to

whether you are utilizing the group, phone calls, and recovery literature for your own recovery. If you are not doing anything for your recovery, you can not heal from these affects. The partner who chooses to do nothing, can become the problem in the relationship later. She might get depressed or still be angry or continue to bring up his shortcomings even years later. Not doing anything for your recovery is the biggest mistake partners of sex addicts make.

I strongly recommend that each partner work through the *Partners Recovery Guide*. This book is designed specifically for partners of sex addicts. It is basically therapy in a box. If you use this book, it will reduce therapy time: It is a behavior you can believe, and *that* will signify that you are in recovery.

Remember that believing behavior works both ways. He is making progress, if he is doing the recovery behaviors and the same applies to you. The happiest ending in my experience of working with couples happens when both work their recovery, so they both can be the best they can be for each other, for the rest of their lives.

20
The Twelve Steps

Now we enter into the recovery program known as the Twelve Steps. The original Twelve Steps were written many years ago for *Alcoholics Anonymous*. These alcoholics, after some period of sobriety, decided to write down the principles and the steps they took to maintain their sobriety and to live a healthier life. These principles and steps have been used throughout the world to help millions of people with various addictions such as narcotic abuse, overeating, emotional problems, co-dependency, and sexual addiction.

**The Twelve Steps of Alcoholics Anonymous
Adapted for Partners**

1. We admitted we were powerless over our sexually addicted partner, and that our lives had become unmanageable.
2. Came to believe that a power greater than ourselves could restore us to sanity.

3. Made a decision to turn our will and our lives over to the care of God, as we understood God.

4. Made a searching and fearless moral inventory of ourselves.

5. Admitted to God, to ourselves, and to another human being the exact nature of our wrongs.

6. Were entirely ready to have God remove all these defects of character.

7. Humbly asked God to remove our shortcomings.

8. Made a list of all persons we had harmed and became willing to make amends to them all.

9. Made direct amends to such people wherever possible, except when to do so would injure them or others.

10. Continued to take personal inventory, and when we were wrong, promptly admitted it.

11. Sought through prayer and meditation to improve our conscious contact with God as we understood God, praying only for knowledge of God's will for us and the power to carry that out.

12. Having had a spiritual awakening as the result of these steps, we tried to carry this message to others, and to practice these principles in all our day to day living.

Note: The Twelve Steps are reprinted and adapted with permission of Alcoholics Anonymous World Services, Inc. Permission to reprint and adapt the Twelve Steps does not mean that AA has reviewed or approved the content of this publication, nor that AA agrees with the views expressed herein. AA is a program of recovery from alcoholism. Use of the Twelve Steps in connection with programs and activities which are patterned after AA, but which addresses other problems, does not imply otherwise.

An Interpretation of the Twelve Steps for Partners of Sex Addicts

What we will attempt to do in the following pages is explain the principles and concepts of the Twelve Steps as they are used for recovery from being a partner of a sexual addict, so that you can implement them in your personal recovery. Our comments here should not be construed as representing any particular Twelve Step fellowship. They are my own interpretation of the steps from my own experience, as well as from years of clinical experience helping partners of sex addicts recover by using the Twelve Step process.

Step One: We admitted we were powerless over our partners sexual addiction and that our lives had become unmanageable.

We. I am so glad that the first word in the first step is "we." I would hate to think "I" was the only person who ever went through this. Being a partner of a sex addict is an international, as well as a national problem. "We" means that we have similar experiences and we share similarities. We grew up in the same family, thousands of miles apart. We had the same kind of partners, sexual experiences, abuses and neglects. *We* is a comforting word in this step. You can see that you are not alone and don't have to be alone. You can get better if you decide to get together. *We* is an encouraging word and is also essential. Without each other, we often fail to recover from the affects of being in a relationship with a sex addict.

Admitted. This is a difficult word. Many of us have had situations in our childhood that we have had to admit.

Maybe we stole something or something happened to us, and we had to admit what we did. Do you remember those feelings of dread before admitting to something? Then we went ahead and admitted it. We told what we did or what happened to us. After we admitted it, we felt less heavy or burdened as if we could now move on. Admitting to the affects from his addiction and now, our own issues, is one of the more difficult things we will do in our recovery. Admitting is a very important aspect of recovery; only those who admit to having issues can move forward in recovery and life.

We Were Powerless. Again, I'm glad that there is a "we" in there; that I'm not the only one who is powerless. When we talk about power, we talk about control. Authority, strength, or force gives us the ability to be over someone else. But that is not what this word is. This word is powerless and as we know, the suffix "less" means without-- like *jobless*. This is a tough reality for every partner. We are without any strength, power, control, or force to influence our partner's addiction. This is why we need each other and a recovery program. Sometimes that is why we need therapy. We are powerless. We have tried not to influence our addict without success.

Our Partners. Being powerless over our sex addict is difficult. Often the attempts to be "more" for him have failed. If we loved him enough, we believed we could change him: It is an erroneous belief.

The fact is he is a sex addict. He was probably a sex addict before you met and will be one (hopefully in recovery). If you didn't cause it, you can't cure it. When we accept this, we assert our powerlessness over our partner's sex addiction.

And That Our Lives. Our lives can be many things.

It can be our physical, emotional, intellectual or spiritual life. If you look at all the parts of our lives, they wouldn't equal the totality of our life. Our lives are the very core of us. It is the inner part of us that identifies us as being separate from another person. This is what has been affected as we look at our affects from his sexual addiction. This is the part that feels disconnected, alone, confused and isolated when our needs are not being met.

Had Become. These two words indicate to me that this has taken a while. It means that it took time, energy, process and choices. It didn't just happen. It took a while and then eventually, it was made. Your life didn't become overwhelming or devastated instantly, but over a period of time.

Unmanageable. When we think about manageable, we think about things being in order, or serene. We can tell, when we walk into a store, whether the store is manageable or unmanageable. This word means unorganized and chaotic. If someone came from the outside and saw this, they would say "What a mess!" Sometimes this is the way we feel, and our feelings can be valid. Our lives, in many of the areas we have talked about, have become unmanageable, unconnected, uncontrollable, and unpredictable. No matter how hard we have tried to make our lives look good or perfect, they are not. Our lives have become empty and hollow in many respects. Now, through Step One, if we can admit this unmanageability, we have a strong hope of recovery.

I encourage everyone to take Step One seriously, because it is the foundation of the **Twelve Step** program. It will cause you to have a good house of recovery to live in for the future.

For further step work on Step One and all of the

Twelve Steps for partners, I encourage you to use the workbook *Beyond Love*. This guide is specifically for partners of sex addicts. This is made available through Heart to Heart Counseling Center, and can be ordered from the back of this book.

Step Two: Came to believe that a power greater than ourselves could restore us to sanity.

Came to Believe. Again, notice the step is written in the past tense. The original steps were written to share the process that the original members of AA went through in recovery. There was a process through which they came to believe.

It is really a simple process. You come to believe many things during your lifetime. For example, you came to believe that there was a Santa Claus. Later you came to believe that there wasn't a Santa Claus. As you grew older, you may have come to believe that a certain person liked you, and, later realized, they didn't like you. We come to believe certain religious and political positions. There is some consistency to this process throughout our lives. In this process, there is a definite point at which you understand or come to believe.

In Twelve Step groups, the process of coming to believe is something that often happens as a result of exposure to other recovering people. You may not necessarily know the date, or the hour, when you did come to believe, but you know that you did feel differently, and you began to have hope. This is so important in recovery, because knowing that you have come to believe, or knowing you do believe can save your life. Partners can get down, feel hopeless or worthless, experience severe shame, and guilt from past traumas, or present circumstances, and resort to sad behaviors of destruction, isolation, or depression. If you have come to believe, you can have hope that God cares for you, loves you, and accepts you.

A Power. "A" is a common word. You use it every day. A cat, a dog, a book--and in every context in which it is used, it denotes one. If you were going to use a word to describe more than one, you would say "these," or another word that indicates plurality. This step is not written in the plural. It says "a" power greater than ourselves. This is significant. Being an "a" here, you realize that there is one entity, one strength, one energy, one spirit, one power. It is significant that, as you come to believe, you are believing in one being.

Greater Than Ourselves. This is one of the first areas which requires trust from the partner. We now know that there is one that is greater than ourself. This is the best news we have in recovery, that we don't have to figure this out alone. As you begin to trust this power, you begin to recover from the sick patterns, poor choices, and undesirable relationships that have been so much a part of your past.

In the original context of AA, this power greater than ourselves indicated that the power was greater than that first group of recovering alcoholics. This one single power was greater than a whole group. That's a lot of power. People in recovery frequently first recognize this power in the group, but in reality it is greater than the group. Even if you had a power greater than yourself, you may have had difficulty accessing the resources of that power and applying them to your life. In the program, you come to believe that this power has more ability to solve life's problems than you do alone. What a relief!

Could. "Could" is one of the most helpful, loving expressions in the Twelve Steps. Could this power have the ability, the resources, the energy, the intention of helping you along in the recovery process? It is possible now to begin to be restored. It is possible now to begin to be healthy, to have loving relationships with loving people, to be loved and nurtured in a healthy way. It can be done, and this power can do it. It is the experience of many partners in recovery that, if given the freedom and the opportunity, if you quit trying to do it all on your own, this power will do for you what you have been unable, or unwilling, to do for yourself. All you have to do is ask.

Restore Us to Sanity. "Restore" means bringing something back. Frequently when you think of restoration, you think of restoring an automobile or an old house, making it look like new. The same is true for those recovering from the affects of his sexual addiction.

Partners have, for so long, been robbed of spirituality, intimacy, trust, and even their own reality. In a world that should have been safe, we were violated, again and again.

Insanity is natural when you live with someone hosting a disease as crazy as sexual addiction. You may have difficulty applying the idea of insanity to yourself, but often having two realities at the same time, and living with the secret, can make most partners feel insane. You try, again and again, to do something that should work, but doesn't. You try, and try, to fix the problems that sexual addiction creates in your life, without success.

The behaviors themselves are insane, but the fact that you continue to use them, never stopping to realize that they're not working, qualifies you to be restored to sanity. It is possible for partners of sex addicts to be restored to sanity. Those already in recovery have experienced it. They are living proof that it is possible to make better choices, and we hope, as you read this, you know that it is possible for you. You may still feel crazy, but if you have gotten this far in your recovery, you have a good chance at finding sanity.

Step Three: Made a decision to turn our wills and our lives over to the care of God, as we understood God.

Made. "Made" is kind of like "became." It indicates a process which involves time and choices, but there is definitely a time when it is done. For example, when kids in school make an ashtray, or a meal or dress in home economics, or a table in shop, there is a time when it is in the process of being made, and then it is completed. It is made. "Made" is something that has been coming along, but is finally resolved to the point that you can say it is done.

A. Here again we come to that little word, "a." It is one. What we are discussing in Step Three is a one time event. Many people want to spread this step out, but as you move along in this process of working the steps, you will see why we only make this decision one time.

Decision. When you make a decision, you list the good and the bad, the pros and cons, of a situation. In this step, you can make a list of what you have done with your life in the past, and how you could deal with your life differently in the future. Such a list makes it easier to make the decision you are asked to make in Step Three. It is a decision.

Compare it to a traditional courtship and marriage. It is like you had an engagement period in Step Two, during which you get to know your power greater than yourself, and you began to get comfortable with the idea of having God in your life. Step Three is the marriage ceremony itself, where you make a commitment to share your life with God. You just have a single ceremony, but it sets the stage for further development through the relationship. Step Three asks you to be willing to share your life with God. The decision is a one time event, but it provides a means for further growth.

To Turn. Turning can be expressed in many ways. Someone said once that turning means to flip over, kind of like a hot cake. The hot cake gets done on one side, and then you have to turn it over.

It is a pretty simple definition of turn, but it is also pretty profound. If you flip over, you make a total change from the way you have been up to this point.
"Turn" is used on highways all over the world to indicate direction: signs may indicate a left or right turn, or U-turn. When you make a U-turn, you turn around and go in the opposite direction. What you do in Step Three is definitely a U-turn! You turn away from your limited understanding of how life should be. You leave behind perceptions, experiences, and ideas about things you thought you understood. You turn from them and gain a whole new perspective. This is an essential part of recovery. You are turning into something, or turning somewhere else, and it is amazing how far that turn can take you, as you continue in your recovery efforts.

Our Will. Again, this is plural, as the group stays and works, together. In this group of safe people, who have turned their wills and lives over to God, you will begin to see this decision as a possibility for yourself. But what is your will? The simplest definition of "will" is probably the ability to make the choices you do for your life. In the group, you will begin to turn over the choices that you make to God. This can be an easy thing for some, but, for others, it can be a very hard thing to do. It means you must turn your choices over to God, try to understand God's perspective, and follow that perspective in your life. That is why Step Three is so powerful.

In many recovery groups there is a phrase called "stinking thinking" which refers to a dysfunctional thought patters that addicts often have. Stinking thinking is the way a non-recovering person thinks. This thinking doesn't work. The choices non-recovering people make don't bring about positive results. There seems to be a certain self-destructiveness to their choices and behavior. Step Three cuts to the core of stinking thinking. It is the beginning of a new life-style.

Giving up their wills is a safety valve. In making decisions about relationships, they are now able to turn to God. As they do, God will demonstrate new directions they can take, and new choices they can make. They will begin getting answers, and will be able to make different choices about their relationship. This is a freedom that is only gained by letting go of will, or sharing the responsibility of *choosing* with God.

Our Lives. Our lives are the result of all our choices. For each individual, life is the totality of all parts. When you turn it all over-spiritually, emotionally, physically, socially, financially and sexually-you give yourself to God. You begin to trust God. You begin to believe that God will take care of you.

You may say: "This is frightening. How can I trust God?!" But simply look at what you have trusted in the past. You have trusted your own ability to think, your own ability to make choices? You have taken the advice of a few chosen people who have not necessarily acted in your best interests.

Turning your will and life over is necessary. It is through this trust experience with God that you begin to believe that God loves you. You begin once again to trust yourself. Eventually, you can even regain your trust in people. Step Three is an essential part of working the steps. It is not a luxury. It is necessary for a healthy, happy life. Working the steps is not always easy, and often you do not understand why you must work them. Often the steps are understood only after they have been completed. Then you realize the beauty of this spiritual process, and open yourself to further growth and joy, as you walk this road with others who are making the same steps toward recovery.

The Care of God. What do you think of when you hear the word "care!" It is often expressed in terms of someone who loves you, someone who demonstrates some kindness toward you, someone who is willing to get in-volved in your life, willing to get in there, and be patient with you, to work with you, and not condemn you in the process; someone who can be nurturing. All these pictures of a loving parent or a loving friend can represent care. Care is felt in the release of energy from one person to another, usually through kind behaviors, like providing a listening ear, or some other sign of concern.

How does this relate to God? What is the care of God? It is simply God's willingness to be involved in a nurturing, supportive, accepting way, in your life. God is concerned for partners of sex addicts. God's concern for others in this world demonstrates that care. You can some-times see it more clearly in the lives of others than you can in your own life. For some partners, the group is a manifestation of the care of God in their lives. It is possible for you, by looking at others in your support group, to connect with this issue in such a way that it radically changes your life. Something as simple as their support can be seen as the extension of God's care and concern.

Now, we'll talk about God. The original writers of the Twelve Steps changed only one word from the initial version. In Step Two they changed the word "God." to "a Power greater than ourselves." That is the only change they made, and it was made for this reason: those first alcoholics said that God was too scary for the recovering person in Step Two. Maybe the recovering person had too many hurts, too many problems with God, so the word was changed to "a Power greater than ourselves" to give the newcomer an engagement period, and allow him or her to experience God through the group's care, nurturing and love. In this way they could come to believe in a caring God who could, and would, help them.

But who is God? Let me share my thoughts with you on this subject. Simply put, God is Love. God is also in authority or in control, especially for those who turn their lives and will over to Him, and switch the authority from themselves to God.

According to what you have learned so far in the steps, God has the ability to restore you. God is more powerful than you are alone, or in a group. God is one who gets actively involved in your life, who has more power, and more success, than you in dealing with the affects of his sexual addiction. This God can and will help you as you work the Twelve Steps.

For many, this understanding of God will develop into a faith that is common in the American culture, and will enable the recovering partner to enjoy the benefits of finding a community that shares the same faith. Some will not. It is a universal blessing of this program, however, that they can, if they are willing, come to a greater relationship with God, as they understand God.

The people who have turned their wills and lives over to the care of a God they understand, who have turned their choices over to God, often have more understanding of how God works, and how God thinks. The group is a good resource, especially for those early in recovery who want an understanding of God. It is very important to realize, as it pertains to understanding God, that no single person is going to understand the totality of God, but the members of your support group can be helpful in this journey.

As We Understood God. One way to interpret this is to compare your understanding of God with the way you function in relationships with people, because we are talking about a relationship. When you first meet someone, your knowledge of him or her is limited. Only through time, communication, and commitment to any relationship, do you really come to understand another person. The same is true in your relationship with God. Coming to understand God is a process which is available to any, and all, in recovery, who are willing to turn their wills and lives over, so that they can experience a new life, a new freedom, and find happiness. The beauty of finding God in the Twelve Steps.

Step Four: Made a searching and fearless moral inventory of ourselves.

Made A Searching. Searching holds the possibility of fun, but for partners, searching can be extremely painful. When you search, you intend to find something. For example, when you lose your keys, you go searching, with the intent of finding the keys. As you begin your inventory, you are searching, scrutinizing, seeking with intent, to find something significant.

In this context, "searching" indicates that you will have to expend some energy. This is the beginning of what is often referred to in the program as the "action steps." You now begin to take action in your own behalf. Note that this step is also in the past tense. As you begin your inventory, you can know that others have passed this way before, have survived, and gotten better. You are not alone.

Fearless. "Fearless" simply means without fear. This is the attitude with which you approach your moral inventory. Being fearless allows you to view your inventory objectively, as you uncover the pain. You will be looking at what was done to you, and what you have done to yourself and others.

Many of the experiences you will be looking at are extremely painful. For some, the painful experience was childhood abuse. Others may have experienced abuse or neglect, including their relationship with the sex addict. For some, it will be something they would much rather not ever remember, something they may think it only imagined. Fearlessness will lead you to look at your own part in the unhealthy relationships you have been in as an adult, and at the patterns that have been repeated in your life. You need to look at these things with an attitude of courage and bravery. You can, because in Step Three you turned your will and life over to the care of a loving God.

Moral. "Moral" can be defined as right and wrong, categories of black and white, or good and bad. Something that is immoral could be defined as something that violates your conscience. As you look at your life in Step Four, you will be looking for things which you've done which have violated your conscience. For example, as children, many of us had the experience of raiding the cookie jar. We knew that we were not supposed to get a cookie. There might not be anything wrong with having a cookie, but we were told not to, so it became wrong. We waited until our parents could not see, and took a cookie anyway. It probably tasted good, but we may have felt badly afterward. We felt badly because we knew we did something wrong.

In Step Four, you will also be looking at how you were violated by others. Have you ever said to yourself, "If they really knew me, they wouldn't like me. If they knew I was sexually abused or that my partner is a sex addict, they wouldn't be my friend." The shame and guilt you carry, from the actions of other people toward you, can be overwhelming. Step Four is designed to release you from that shame and guilt as you look at how your moral code has been violated by others.

It is wrong to believe that you are unworthy because of your past. In recovery, you come to know yourself and let others know you. Step Four is about coming to know yourself, being honest with yourself about what happened, taking into account how it affected your life, and where it leaves you today. In short, Step Four is an inventory. You will list everything that happened, even if it involved others and you were simply an innocent bystander, as in the case of the divorce of a parent.

Such an event may not have had anything to do with your morality, but it did affect you emotionally.

Inventory. What are you to inventory in Step Four? You inventory your experiences because, as a human being, that is what you have on hand. You inventory your memory, for that is what you have been given to record your experiences. Many see this inventory as a life story. It is a process where you begin to see the truth of what you've done, and what has been done to you. Some things will be negative, others will be positive. When a storekeeper takes inventory, he lists not only the things he wants to get rid of, but the things he wants to keep. And he doesn't just make a mental note of it; he writes it down.

Step Four is a written assignment. You will need to have pen or pencil, paper, and a quiet place where you can be uninterrupted. Some just begin writing. Some organize their inventory by ages, such as birth-to six years, six to twelve years, and so on. Still others have done it by first listing all the traumatic events they can remember--things that were done to them, or by them, that violated their value system, then writing how they felt at the time, and how they feel now, about those events. There is no right or wrong way to write an inventory. The important thing is just to do it. You will be face to face, for perhaps the first time with the total reality of your life. It can be pretty overwhelming, so don't be afraid to let your sponsor or therapist know how you are feeling while writing your inventory. As you transfer your story to paper, you are also transferring the pain, guilt and shame onto paper. Writing an inventory can be a very positive, transforming experience, and it is vital to your recovery from the affects of his sex addiction.

Of Ourselves. Once again, you can see this is plural. You can know that others have done this before. You can survive the pain of writing your inventory down. It is joyous to see others freed from their shame. As you see other members of your support groups complete their inventories, you will begin to believe that this release from shame can happen for you too. You are reminded that only you can do this for yourself. Only you know your pain, the strength of your fears, your deepest secrets. Only you are qualified to write this inventory. Now is the time to decide for yourself who you are, and who you want to be. There is great freedom in taking your focus off what is wrong with others, and doing a searching and fearless moral inventory of yourself. You may not understand the value of this step until you have completed it, but it is well worth the pain and tears.

Step Five: Admitted to God, to ourselves, and to another human being the exact nature of our wrongs.

Admitted. Here you are again, looking at that word, "admitted." You already know that it means to "fess up," or acknowledge what is already true. You may have already experienced the pain and joy of doing this, probably as a child or adolescent. Perhaps you put yourself in a situation you knew your parents would not approve, or did something wrong, and knew you were going to have to tell them, because you knew they were going to find out anyway. Do you remember your feelings of guilt and shame, like you had let yourself and them down? Then you somehow got the courage to tell them what you had done. You admitted the truth--no matter the consequences. It felt better, finally, to let the secret out.

The same is true in Step Five. You admit all that you have written in your Fourth Step. You let out all those secrets and finally feel that clean joy which comes from truly being totally known.

To God. God might be the easiest person to tell, or the hardest, depending on your relationship with Him. If you feel God has let you down before, admitting what has been wrong in your life can be particularly difficult. Fortunately, God is forgiving of all that you have done, and is willing to restore any lost part of yourself. As one wise person in recovery stated, "It's okay to tell God. God already knows it all anyway, and is just waiting for us to be honest about it, too."

To Ourselves. Admitting your past secrets to yourself often takes place as you write your Fourth Step, if you are truly fearless and thorough when writing it. Admitting your powerlessness, your need to be restored to sanity, your profound amazement at your poor choices, and your sincere sense of having failed yourself, is probably the most humbling experience you will have regarding your sense of who you are.

It is at this point, though, that the recovery of your true self is able to take an upward turn, without the overwhelming sense of shame or guilt that has been so closely bound to you in the past. You are now able to begin a more shame-free life, which empowers you to experience the next, and most essential, part of this step: being able to reveal yourself to another human being.

And to Another Human Being. "What? I have to tell all this stuff to somebody else, face to face?" Yes, telling your story to another human being is the most crucial part of your recovery. In writing your Fourth Step, you have taken your total history of shame, hurt, abandonment, abuse, acting-out, and poor choices, and poured it consciously into one place. Your Fourth Step may even have brought to your conscious awareness some things you have been suppressing for years, and now all of these memories are in one place. If all this pain is kept inside you, and is not shared with another human being, you may talk yourself into believing once again that you are unlovable, or unacceptable, with such a painful, messy past. You could use this negative information and history for condemnation, instead of healing. That is why we must tell another person. We must realize that we are loved and accepted, even though we have been places and experienced things of which we are not proud.

In this Fifth Step you experience spiritually, emotionally, and often physically, a cleansing or a lightening of your load. As you share who you have been, and what you have experienced, with another trusted person, you are reassured that nothing you have done makes you unlovable. Now someone knows the whole truth, and still loves you. It is remarkable!

A note of caution is appropriate here: When you choose someone to hear your Fifth Step, it is important to pick the least condemning, most loving and accepting person you know. You might choose a therapist, sponsor, or spiritual person you trust. Choose someone who understands that you are digging into your past, in order to make your present and future better, someone who will of your support group as well. This choice is yours. Make it in your best interest.

The Exact Nature of Our Wrongs. The fact that this part of the step is so specific will help two kinds of people: those who say, "I can't be specific, so I'll never really feel loved," and those who believe that they can own everybody else's wrongs, and avoid looking at their own choices. The first person needs to be specific in sharing her story, because the shame she experiences about the past is not shame you for your past. This person can be a member tied to specific episodes. We must talk about those specific episodes to relieve the shame associated with them. The second person needs to acknowledge her own shortcomings and "clean her own side of the street," not anyone else's, so that she, too, can be freed from her own shame.

It's a recognized fact that you can't free anyone else from her shame. Each person has to work her own program of recovery, in order to have the kind of happy and fulfilling life we are all capable of experiencing.

Step Six: *Were entirely ready to have God remove all these defects of character.*

Were Entirely Ready. As you move from Step One through Step Five, you discover a process through which you recognize powerlessness, find a God of your understanding, go inside yourself by writing an inventory, and let someone else know who you really are. The very core of the program is in the first five steps. By working these steps you have learned to "trust God and clean house."

Now that you have cleaned house, you must learn how to maintain your new surroundings. It is one process to clean a dirty house, whether you got it dirty yourself or just inherited all the mess and it is another thing entirely to make sure that it never gets dirty again. That is what Step Six and the following steps are all about--preventative maintenance.

You start by "being entirely ready." This simply means that you are 100 percent ready to look at the damage that was done by all that trash, and you evaluate what you can throw away. You might be quite attached to some of that stuff. Even though it doesn't work any longer, you hesitate to give it up. Someday, some of those old behaviors might come in handy, you keep thinking. You forget that each time you try old behavior it causes great pain. "Were entirely ready" indicates that you are finally tired of the pain. You finally realize that changing is not quite as frightening as staying the same.

To Have God. Having God in our lives is so significant for partners of sex addicts. Here, in Step Six, they are reminded that they, like everyone, are blessed by having a relationship with God. They are beginning to believe that God does want the best for them, and that God wants their lives to express this new way of feeling and believing about themselves. God is willing to work with you, as you continue your efforts at recovery.

Remove All. This sounds like an unrealistic, maybe even painful, statement, at least from a human standpoint. "Remove" indicates loss. Partners have certainly experienced loss in their lives. But to lose, or remove, all of their defects? How?

Well, it isn't up to you to decide how, it's only up to you to be ready. Remember that earlier you recognized that you don't have a whole lot of power of your own. In Step Six you will rely on God to have the power to change you.

Defects Of Character. As you consider the term, "defects of character," you might be thinking of some of the ways you have behaved, and felt that didn't work very well. Go ahead, get a pencil and paper, and write down what comes to mind. Reviewing your inventory should give you a good idea of things about your character you might want changed.

For example, perhaps the way you express your anger indicates a defect of character. Maybe the way you control, and try to manipulate, your spouse or children, or the way you pout to get your own way, or isolate, or run away from responsibility for yourself, are things you want to change. Honesty is important in listing these defects, because the ones you hold on to will keep you stuck in old patterns, and you will continue to attract unhealthy people into your life, especially in intimate relationships.

It is the experience of recovering partners that, as they become more healthy and honest themselves, they gravitate toward more healthy, honest people, and are better able to determine who is unhealthy. Understanding this can certainly motivate you to really look at your defects of character, and be 100 percent willing to have God remove them. This is the real release that prevents the dust and trash from resettling in your house.

Step Seven: Humbly asked God to remove our shortcomings.

Humbly. Many struggle with the word, "humble," having been humiliated, time and again, by his sexual addiction. Humility is not the same as humiliation, although you may feel something like humiliation as you see the devastation in your own life, and the lives of those around you, caused by your defects of character. Humility, in this case, means recognizing your true humanity. You see in Step Seven the manner with which you should approach God. Humility means knowing that you don't have the power to change yourself, but that God does. You come into God's presence with a humble heart, but with hope as well. And, as you ask, you shall receive. As long as you don't have preconceived ideas of just how, and when, God will remove your defects of character, you will have them removed.

Asked God. Humility requires that we ask, not tell, God anything. By now perhaps you have come to believe that God really does want the best for you; wants you to be free of your defects of character; wants you to feel good about yourself, and to be attracted to healthy people. You are asking, in a sense, to do God's will.

To Remove Our Shortcomings. In Step Six you
became ready. Now you push the "Go" button, and ask God
to take your defects of character, or shortcomings. It would
be nice if it happened all at once, but, again, you will experience it as a process. In this process, God will be with you
throughout your life, removing your shortcomings as you
continue to identify them when they surface, as long as you
are willing to ask for help.

For some partners, this step comes easily. For
others, it is very hard, especially if you are holding onto, still
rationalizing, still defending, still gripping, your defense
mechanisms. In that case, Step Seven can be a painful
experience. As someone once said in a meeting, "There was
never anything I let go of, that didn't have claw marks all
over it, including my defects of character."

You can trust that if you ask, God will remove your
defects of character, no matter how much you resist. If you
decide to hold on to them, you will be fighting a losing
battle. It is at this point that you will really need your
support group. They will give you valuable feedback about
any shortcomings they see you holding on to. If you aren't
sure, ask questions. They will also give you support as you
try new behaviors, in place of the old ones that kept you so
unhappy. Allow them to support you in this growth process.

***Step Eight: Made a list of all persons we had harmed,
and became willing to make amends to them all.***

Made A List. You probably don't have any problem
shopping for groceries if you've made a list. You know that
the most efficient way to shop is to have a written list,
instead of just mental notes, because otherwise you are
likely to get home, and find you have forgotten some essen-

tial items. There is a saying in Alcoholics Anonymous that you should be fearless and thorough from the very start. This is true in Step Eight. Again, take a pencil and paper in hand, and, looking at your inventory, make a list of all those you have harmed. This list should include yourself, as well as others, and can also include what damage was done, and the person's name.

Of All Persons. Here again is that sometimes scary word: all. "All" means every single one. You are, once again, being challenged to be honest. To the degree that you can be honest in making this list, you will have hope for new relationships with important people in your life.

We Had Harmed. It takes an honest person to look at her life, and see the people she has harmed. It is often easier to see how you have been harmed by others. In Steps Four and Five, you looked at how you have been hurt by trusted people in your life; how you have been traumatized; how you have been emotionally abandoned; and how you have suffered. But if all you look at is how you have been harmed, you are only halfway healed.

Just as it can be painful for a recovering alcoholic to see how his drinking damaged those around him, so it can be painful for the recovering partner to realize what she has done to hurt others. For many partners, it is much more comfortable to be the victim. As a matter of fact, they have often been the victim of their own behaviors, of their own past, and even of recent relationships. But past victimization by others just makes it that much more difficult for these people to realize that they have actually harmed other people. The "me acting-out" behavior is just the start of this list. The harm can be very subtle. You need to really search your mind and heart, in order to complete your healing.

And Became Willing. The past tense here reminds

you, one more time, that the hard work demanded in the previous steps is survivable. Partners have worked their way through these steps before, and have found peace and happiness on the other side. It also indicates a process. Recovery doesn't just happen overnight. Becoming willing takes time for everyone, especially if they are holding on to a victim status.

To Make Amends. What does it mean to make amends? For partners, or anyone in recovery for that matter, to make amends means to acknowledge the wrong they have done, and be willing to be different. You stop blaming the other person to justify your own behavior. You stop rationalizing and defending yourself. You stop avoiding responsibility. You continue to change in your relationships with yourself and others. You take full responsibility for what you have done, and to whom you have done it, at least on paper at this point, even if *you're* wrong is less than their wrong.

To Them All. Here is that word "all" again. It seems to appear everywhere throughout the steps. By now your list should include everyone who has in any way been harmed by your actions or lack of actions. You should have found the willingness to be different with each person on that list, including yourself. No stone should be left unturned at this point, or you will still carry old guilt that will keep you stuck in old sick patterns of thinking and relating. With names, phone numbers, and accounts of damages in hand, you are ready to move on.

Step Nine: Made direct amends to such people wherever possible, except when to do so would injure them or others.

Made Direct Amends. In Step Eight, you made your list. Now you go to the "grocery store." In Step Nine, you actually go to the people on your list and make direct amends to them for the inappropriate attitudes or behaviors you have had in the past that have affected them. Notice again that this step is written in the past tense. These steps were written in the late 1930s when the first members of Alcoholics Anonymous became sober. Working these steps, especially Step Nine, was something they had to do to maintain their sobriety, so they would not have to carry the pain, shame, or guilt of the past, or present, into their new sober lives.

They had to be honest with themselves. So do you, as you go to each person on your list and ask them for their forgiveness. When you acknowledge how your behavior affected your relationships with them, you will find incredible freedom. Tremendous emotional weights can be lifted, often relationships can be restored, as the result of working Step Nine. This is not a 100 percent guarantee, since some relationships will remain fractured. However, at least your side of the street will be clean.

You will begin to feel wholeness and happiness in your life, now that you have made the effort to vent completely, without expectations. This is a significant point: You do not make amends with the expectation that your friends or family will change their behavior. You do not make amends with the expectation that people will respond in any certain way. People may, in fact, respond when you make amends, but it is by no means the motivation for you to do what you must rid yourself from what you have been carrying for so long. Inflated expectations can cause you much pain, because others are not always in the same place with their recovery that you are with yours. Many people do not choose a path of recovery at all. Your personal efforts and behavior however, can challenge them into this kind of recovery at some point in the future.

It is not a given that the other person will ask forgiveness in return, even though they may have injured you much more than you have injured them. Your goal is to clean your own slate. You are not responsible for what others leave undone, nor can their shortcomings keep you from recovering and feeling good about yourself.

Except When To Do So Would Injure Them or Others. When you get to this point, you may become confused when you attempt to decide if making amends will injure the person involved, or be detrimental to other, possibly innocent people. Such confusion is best resolved with the assistance of a group, sponsor, or therapist. Confusion is not to be used, however, as an excuse to not make any amends, because you don't want to experience the pain or shame of admitting your past behavior.

What you must consider when admitting past behavior is whether or not your confession would so significantly damage the other person involved that you should not raise the issue to them. You can ask yourself, "Would this be damaging?" If you have a question, do not assume you have the answer. You could very possibly avoid an amend which could restore a relationship, or hold on to an amend that will set you up for old behavior. Go over your list with a sponsor, support group, or therapist, if at all possible.

Step Ten: Continued to take personal inventory and when we were wrong, promptly admitted it.

Continued. Here again you must deal with the maintenance of your newly clean house. You are not letting the dust fall. You are not letting the dirt collect, or the garbage overflow in the can. Here you are in a process, as in Steps Four and Five. Today, when you have been inappropriate or have violated anyone's boundaries, including your own, you don't have to wait five or ten years to make amends. You can do it as you go along.

To Take Personal Inventory. Taking a daily personal inventory is a process in which partners are able to look at each person in their life, and see how they are interacting with this person. They look at their attitudes toward others and honestly evaluate them. This is not done to the point where they are unable to enjoy interactions, but it is an honest evaluation of how they respond to peers, family, and in all other relationships. It also is a reminder that they inventory only their own behavior, not anyone else's.

And When We Were Wrong, Promptly Admitted It. You will be wrong. This part of Step Ten says, "When," not, "If," you were wrong. Many partners have been wronged, but there will still be times when you will be wrong yourself. It is so important for the recovering person to stay free, and not enter into a place of guilt and shame, which can push you into some acting out behavior. So, in the maintenance of Step Ten, when you are wrong, you promptly admit it. "Promptly" is significant because it keeps you from holding on to the baggage, thinking for months about whether you were or weren't wrong. Promptly means admit it right now, right here. If you have been acting inappropriately, say, "I'm sorry. Forgive me, I'm acting inappropriately." It is as simple as that. Step Ten gives you a way to stay free from the bondage of guilt and shame. It keeps you humble, which often helps you to remain healthy.

Step Eleven: Sought through prayer and meditation to improve our conscious contact with God as we understood God, praying only for knowledge of God's will for us and the power to carry that out.

Sought Through Prayer and Meditation. This step not only tells you what you are doing, but it also tells you how to do it. You are seeking. You are looking to improve your relationship with God. This step tells you to do that through prayer and meditation. Prayer is that verbal, and sometimes internal, communication with God. It is such a positive experience for the partner to become more aware of God in her life. This step lets you know that it is your responsibility. Seeking requires action on your part. You may have felt abandoned by God, since you put no real effort into trying to find out where He was. It has been said many times in meetings, "If you can't find God, guess who moved." You move away from God, God never moves away from you. Seeking Him is all that it takes to find Him.

Meditation is a sometimes deeper sense of prayer. Prayer is requesting, asking, interacting. Meditation is listening and hearing God's voice. Many experience rest and peace through meditation, and are able to still the constant obsessive thinking that prevents them from hearing what God has to say: that they are significant, they are loved, and they deserve to be healthy. Meditate on God's character, on your personal relationship with Him, on some scripture or recovery material you have, and allow them to really sink in to your spirit. Be still, and God will speak to you.

To Improve Our Conscious Contact With God. Most partners, like many people, have an unconscious contact with God. They rely most of the time on their own thinking and resources, and connect with God only after they have thoroughly botched their lives. Step Eleven reminds you to keep God in your conscious mind. You are then able to experience the power and love of God in a whole new way. As a result, you will experience life in a whole new way. You will have a higher sense of purpose and joy. The result of this new awareness of God, on a moment to moment basis, is a better relationship with God. As with any relationship, efforts at improving the relationship requires time, energy, and some sort of communication. With time, you will find the method of communication that works best for you. There is no right or wrong way to do it. Just do it.

As We Understood God. It is impossible for any one of us to totally understand God. Indeed, my understanding of God might not work for you, nor yours for me. The beauty of the program is that you can begin to see evidence of God, in other people. Remember this is not a job you undertake on your own. You come to a new understanding of God as you interact with the people in your support group, church, or other community of people seeking knowledge of God. As you listen, you will grow in understanding through other people's experiences of God in their lives.

Praying Only For Knowledge of God's Will For Us. By now you are beginning to see the benefits of letting go of self will. In Step Eleven, you are gently reminded that when you pray for God's will in your life, you are asking for the absolute best solution to whatever you are facing. So often, we push and push situations to turn out the way we want them to, only to find out that we got second, or third, or seventh, or tenth best. It is a very positive thing to realize that you can trust God to have your best interests at heart. The people, places, and things you have given your will over to in the past did not have your best interests at heart. You now trust God enough to say, "Not my will, but thy will be done."

And The Power to Carry That Out. You pray for knowledge of God's will, not just for the sake of having the information, but also for the power to carry it out. Having the information without the willingness or power to carry it out, will not change anything. After prayer for the knowledge, you can now listen in meditation for God to tell you the things you need to do. Sometimes a path will open, sometimes God will bring to mind a defect of character that is getting in your way, and sometimes God will challenge you in the way you are behaving, through intuitive thoughts or feelings you may have. Often the power, to make the changes God seems to want you to make, comes through the people in your support groups. It can even come from seeing someone stuck in old behaviors. You can be motivated to change by seeing the consequences others are experiencing because of their unwillingness to act differently. Once having asked for direction and listened for guidance, you can act with assurance, knowing that if you are on the wrong track, you will come to know it. And you always know that you're not alone.

Step Twelve: Having had a spiritual awakening as the result of these steps, we tried to carry this message to others and to practice these principles in all our day-to-day living.

Having Had A Spiritual Awakening As The Result Of These Steps. It is no wonder that an individual who comes to the steps, and in the process of time admits to powerlessness, the frailty of being human, the need for a relationship with God, actively pursues that relationship, cleans house, makes amends, and maintains this behavior-and has a spiritual awakening. This spiritual awakening is the purpose of working the steps. It is an awakening in which the partner discovers she has worth and value, that she is loved by God, and can be loved by others, if she will only believe in her lovableness and open up her heart and let that love in.

This awakening to a spiritual connection with God can give partners the power to change their way of relating to themselves and the world. They can now see themselves as precious children of a loving God, and treat themselves, and others, accordingly.

We Tried to Carry This Message to Others. In the beginning of Alcoholics Anonymous, it was not a matter of a drunk alcoholic seeking advice and support from someone who was sober. It was the recovering alcoholic who sought out the active drinker. Bill W., the cofounder of AA, knew that if he couldn't share what he had discovered about his relationship with God and its importance to his sobriety, he wouldn't be able to stay sober. This is true for partners of sex addicts, too. As they progress in their recovery, and become less absorbed in their own pain, they will begin to see opportunities to share their experiences, strength, and hope with other partners who are suffering from the same low self esteem, dependency or independency problems, and lack of boundaries that you experienced. And they will share, not to get them well, but to remain mindful of the miracle of recovery in their own lives. Without constant reminders, they are likely to forget where their strength and health come from, and become complacent.

One of the truest sayings around recovery groups is, "You can't keep it, if you don't give it away." The door to recovery is opened to you, because others passed this way before. It is your joy, as well as your responsibility, to keep the door open for those who follow you, and lead them to the door if they can't find it. It is the only way to ensure freedom for all.

And To Practice These Principles In All Our Day-To-Day Living. Here is the most practical part of the Twelve Steps. Take what you have learned, and keep doing it every day. Practice admitting your powerlessness over the problems in your life. Practice acknowledging God's ability to run your life and keep you from practicing old behaviors. Practice new thinking and behavior skills. Practice prayer and meditation. Like the athlete who must exercise daily to stay in shape, you need to practice daily the new skills you have learned, so you can stay in good emotional and spiritual shape. It took many years of practicing old behaviors for you to end up with such low self esteem and such a lack of boundaries. It will take practice to become the new person you want to be. But it is possible!

Congratulations to all who embark on this journey of the Twelve Steps. These steps, when followed, are a tried and true path toward healing from the affects of a relationship with a sex addict. You may not have caused the pain, but you are the one now responsible to heal your pain from his addiction. The partners I have counseled, that are most successful in this healing process, are those who actively worked the Twelve Steps.

21
Professional Counseling

In addition to the vital attendance and involvement in Twelve Step recovery, many partners benefit greatly from professional therapy.

"What? Am I in need of therapy, too?" Does the idea of therapy frighten you? A general discussion of the types of therapy available might help you decide if therapy is for you.

Like the medical or financial fields, the mental health field has various levels of professionally trained people. These professionals have a wide variety of philosophies and training perspectives, and can meet the different needs partners of sex addicts have.

Psychiatrist

Psychiatrists are medical doctors. They attend several years of medical school, and are trained to look at biological reasons for problems with the human being. They are trained in medications that influence the chemistry of the brain. This professional can be a valuable help or support the partner if the addict has been previously diagnosed with a disorder of depression, manic-depression, or other problem that requires the supervision of a medical doctor. He or she can prescribe medication the partner might need to feel better, such as antidepressant medication.

If the psychiatrist has had addiction training, or has had exposure to workshops dealing with the affects of sexual addiction, he or she may be of some help to you, as you work on your issues of recovery from the affects of your partner's addiction.

Psychologist

A psychologist is quite different from a psychiatrist, although they are often confused, as they both have the designation of doctor. Psychologists are Ph.D., Ed.D., or Psy.D.'s, not medical doctors. They have not attended and graduated from medical school. They are not licensed physicians. Therefore, they cannot prescribe medication. They spend their educational training looking at the cognitive, or thinking, aspects of the human being, such as Intelligence Quotient, reading and math levels, psychological testing, and the like. He or she is often trained to do individual, group, and marital therapy.

A psychologist, with a doctorate in psychology, can be of great help to the partner, especially if the psychologist has had experience working with sex addicts and their partners. A psychologist can be of help in therapy to a partner, particularly if the partner is experiencing a psychological problem, such as depression, suicidal thoughts, or a compulsive eating, sleeping, or alcohol disorder. Often these survival mechanisms respond well to treatment under the care of a trained and licensed psychologist.

Licensed Professional Counselor

The Licensed Professional Counselor, or L.P.C., usually has either masters level training, or Ph.D. level training with expertise in counseling or another field, i.e., sociology or anthropology. They can acquire a counselor's license through taking certain counseling classes. A master's level degree is the minimum required for the L.P.C. in most states. The master's level professional may also have a degree in an area other than counseling, like an M.Ed. (Master's in education), and take a prescribed number of classes in counseling during, or after, completing a graduate degree program, to acquire a professional license from the state he or she practices. This is something to note in your initial interview with a Licensed Professional Counselor. You can ask exactly what his or her background is, because some licenses may not require a degree in counseling in some states. This is important for partners to know when they are seeking help for their own issues, or for the issues regarding their family, marriage, or children.

The master's level L.P.C., much like a psychologist, can be a great resource for a partner as she deals with family and individual problems. An L.P.C. is usually able to identify and deal with depression, obsessive/compulsive disorders, addictive disorders, co-dependency, and other issues.

L.P.C.'s, like psychiatrists and psychologists, have ongoing training and, in most states, will have a more reasonable fee structure for those seeking counseling. In finding a Licensed Professional Counselor, ask how many years they have been practicing, and review the "Questions to Ask" section at the end of this chapter, to determine the

183

counselor's experience with treatment for both the addict and the partner.

Social Workers

Social workers will have either a Bachelor's, or a Master's, level education. They may have several levels of certification which can differ from state to state. They may be a Certified Social Worker (CSW) or a Masters level Social Worker (MSSW), depending on their experience. Their training is mostly from a social perspective. Seeing issues from a social perspective is beneficial, and can be helpful, but unless specific training is given to the Social Worker in the field of addictions, there may be limits as to how helpful this professional can be.

However, if there is a need for social services for the family, or for the sex addict, for example, in finding places for residential treatment, a social worker can usually be quite resourceful. In some states the social worker is much like a Licensed Professional Counselor, as they provide individual, group, or family therapy. In other states and situations, they may do social histories and things of that nature. In finding a social worker, you will need to find out what educational training and experience they have had. You may find that this will be a very beneficial relationship to you, as you seek help, for either your own issues, or those of your family. Again, refer to the "Questions to Ask" section at the end of this chapter for further information.

Pastoral Counselors

Pastoral counseling is also available in many areas. Pastoral counselors include people who have professional degrees in counseling from an accredited seminary or institution. They may have a Doctoral level education (Ph.D.), or they may have Master's level education. Pastors of local congregations would be included in this category. Although most pastors minimally have a Bachelor's level education, some may have no formal education at all. Such counselors can be significantly helpful to those who have strong church, Christian, or religious backgrounds. Pastoral counselors can be very helpful in your recovery, because development of spirituality is a significant part of recovery for the whole person.

The strengths of a pastoral counselor would include spiritual training, coupled with professional experience and professional training in the fields of addictions, or counseling and psychological training. With such training, a pastoral counselor could be of the utmost benefit.

Some possible weaknesses of the pastoral counselor might be a lack of training or skill in some areas. The pastor who has had no training in counseling, may be of brief support to the partner of a sex addict, but might not be as beneficial in resolving personal issues, or identifying other psychological problems that she might have. Pastors are usually not trained counselors, but can be a great support to the partner of a sex addict in the recovery process.

The pastoral counselor, like all other professionals discussed, should be asked the appropriate questions from the "Questions to Ask" section. This is very important. Often, their understanding of addictions and sexual issues can influence how therapeutic their service can be.

Christian Counseling

Christian counseling is another form of counseling which is now readily available in most larger cities, as well in some smaller communities. Christian counseling is not exactly the same as pastoral counseling. Many Christian counselors do not hold a position as a pastor, nor will they have professional pastoral counselor education training.

A Christian counselor is often professionally trained in the theory of counseling, psychology, and human development. These counselors can be Master's or Doctoral level trained professionals, but the training that the counselor receives can vary widely. It is wise to check the Christian counselor's training prior to engaging in any therapeutic relationship.

There is a specific benefit in having a Christian counselor for those who embrace the Christian faith. They can be a great source of help, especially if they are able to integrate biblical truths and biblical understanding into the healing process. They can be very supportive and encouraging to the personal development of the partner, and can also facilitate growth for the whole family. Again, ask the questions relating to training and expertise in the area of sex addiction. Just because they are a Christian does not guarantee they understand, or successfully treat, the affects of sex addiction.

Certified Alcohol and Drug Addiction Counselors or Licensed Chemical Dependency Counselors

CADAC's and LCDC's are available in most areas, although their designations may differ from state to state. These are counselors with a variety of training backgrounds.

They may have a Ph.D., a Master's or Bachelor's degree, or may have had no formal education whatsoever. Again, the training of an individual counselor is very significant. This cannot be stressed more, than in the field of alcohol and drug addictions. In some states individuals recovering from alcoholism or drug addiction, who want to enter the helping profession, find that such certification is the easiest way into this field. They do have a valid experience and understanding of the addiction process, as well as understanding of the recovery process. However, caution must be used, in that recovering people often have multiple addiction problems. This is something to be noted when interviewing an addictions counselor. In addition, it is important to ask how they have integrated a Twelve Step philosophy into their own lives. Unless a counselor has completed at least a Fourth and Fifth Step and has begun the process of making amends, his or her perceptions might still be clouded by guilt and shame, and the counselor might not be able to facilitate the growth you need in your life.

Addiction counselors do have some strengths, however. They are often trained in family systems theory. They are familiar with the dynamics of addiction and usually come from a Twelve Step perspective. Often these counselors can be found working in alcohol and drug addiction treatment centers. Sometimes they share an office with a psychiatrist, psychologist, or master's level counselor. They are often supervised in their work by a degreed professional. You can ask if the case load is being supervised, and by whom, and what that supervision process is. This is important, because some supervisors, due to time constraints, will not review each case thoroughly. Another benefit to an addictions counselor, is that he or she would be aware of recovery groups in the area and the importance of support groups.

Marriage and Family Counselors

Marriage and Family Counselors can have a variety of degrees in education also. They may have a Ph.D., or a Master's degree in marriage and family counseling. For partners, this may or may not be helpful, depending on the situation. If you are in a marriage or a committed relationship, such a counselor can be very beneficial.

Marriage and family counselors come from a family systems approach, taking into consideration the needs of the entire family, and not just the needs of one person. Also, they will be highly attuned to how each family member processes problems, and how the family members interact with each other.

For example, in some addictive systems, the addict is the one who is perceived as needing help, the wife is the one who is strong and "helps" the addict, while the children are her supporters, her cheerleaders in helping Dad. From a systems approach, a counselor might observe this family dysfunction and point out, "Dad appears to need to be sick, so that Mom can be a helper to him." Mom now needs to give up the helper role and establish her own identity and boundaries, so if Dad recovers, the family doesn't need somebody else to be sick, i.e., the children or Mother herself.

The marriage and family counselor will be highly astute in these matters and can be beneficial to the partner of a sex addict, as well as to the family as a whole. Refer to the "Questions to Ask" section to determine what training and experience this counselor has in addictions, in general, and, in sexual addiction, specifically, as well as in recovery from the affects of sexual addiction.

It is very appropriate to interview the professional

you are considering as a therapist. Each addict has a different history, and could have possible conflicts with certain professionals due to their past experiences. Also, the many professionals discussed here represent a sort of continuum of care. At one point in recovery, you might find one type of professional more helpful than another. Many practices include several types of therapists, and are able to treat partners and sex addicts from what is known as a multidisciplinary view. In interviewing a potential therapist, consider the following list of questions.

Questions to Ask

- [ ] Do you have experience working with partners of sex addicts?
- [ ] How many sex addicts and their partners have you counseled in the last two months?
- [ ] Do you have training to do therapy with people with addictions and their families? (State or Board certification)
- [ ] Are you a recovering person working a Twelve Step program?
- [ ] What books have you read on sexual addiction and their partners?
- [ ] Do you have specific training to deal with (if these issues apply to you) rape victims, survivors of child sexual abuse, incest or other trauma?

Telephone Counseling

The current number of professionals who treat partners of sex addicts specifically, and, with a great deal of success, can be limited-even in the larger metropolitan area.

Heart to Heart Counseling Center has established telephone counseling for the sex addict, his partner, and for couple counseling.

We have seen the same success rates for clients using telephone counseling, as those who come into the office. More information can be found at the back of the book on this service. This form of counseling is especially helpful for those who travel quite a bit, because they can call for their appointment from anywhere, and speak to the same counselor every week. Telephone counseling is also helpful to those who feel that their confidentiality is of utmost importance. We see many physicians, lawyers, ministers, businessmen and students who don't want to run into their counselor at the grocery store. They also don't have to walk into his office where they may be seen by someone they may know. Some like it because they don't have to locate a baby-sitter to go to an appointment.

For whatever reason, using the phone for counseling, has been very successful for the recovery process.

3-Day Intensives

Three-Day Intensives are offered out of our offices in Colorado Springs, Colorado. Miracles often happen for couples during this three day period. Three sessions are scheduled for couples each day, for three days (two sessions for individual intensives). This is a great way to get a lot of recovery work done in a very short amount of time. For more information, see our appendix for quotes from previous attendees of our 3-Day Intensives.

22
Groups

During the healing process, many partners find it helpful to attend support groups to expedite their recovery. Groups can be a great asset to the partner of a sex addict. I can't tell you how many partners over the years have told me how important their support group was during their healing process.

There are basically two types of groups for partners who want to heal from the affects of his sex addiction. The first of these is the traditional Twelve Step support group and the second group is what we call a Partner's Group.

The traditional Twelve Step groups that exist are s-anon, COSA and CoSLAA. Each of these groups are for partners of sex addicts, and will have partners in them who basically understand, from one degree or another, where you have been and the hurt you may have been through.

Some of these are very strong groups with good role models. The groups that reflect strength are those where they actually work their Twelve Steps individually and in group settings. Group members call one another for support during the week and utilize sponsor relationships. The partners in the group meetings stay focussed on recovery. A strong Twelve Step group, regardless of which group it is, will help partners tremendously during recovery.

The type of Twelve Step groups to be weary of are characterized by these behaviors.

1. Not actively working the Twelve Steps individually, or as a group.
2. Meetings feel like male bashing sessions instead of focussing on partner issues.
3. Group members do not have sponsors.
4. The phone does not seemed to be used by the group members.
5. There is no mention of partners acting-out, or slips, during the meetings.

These groups may mean well, but long term can allow you to stay in the problem instead of moving toward the solution. In almost any Twelve Step group, you can find a few members who are really working the program. Find the winners, and stay with them. Even in the worst of groups, you can still try to do your own work.

I have seen transformation happen in partners lives as they attend Twelve Step support groups. I believe these groups can be of great help for you in your recovery process. The contact information for these groups is located in the Appendix of this book, as well as on our links page at www.sexaddict.com.

The second type of group is what we call a Partners Group. There are some major differences between a Partner's Group and a traditional Twelve Step Group. The first major difference is that you do not have to be co-dependent to be a member of the Partners Group. You can be healthy, or you can be unhealthy, due to the damage of his sex addiction, or previous life wounds. The second major difference is that this is a work group, you and all members of the group are expected to report in to the group the exercises you have completed in the *Partners Recovery Guide* and *Beyond Love*.

The first part of a Partners Group is checking in. "Hi. This is Barbara. I am a partner of a sex addict. This week I have completed exercises #34 through #37 in the *Partners Recovery Guide,* and I am working on Step Three in *Beyond Love*." This creates a very positive momentum in the group.

The person who wants to stay in the problem will be obvious to the group and to herself by her lack of work. The people, who are doing the work, naturally become the leaders, instead of the strongest personality taking over. The group sessions for the Partners Group are basically in three sections.

1. Check in on your progress
2. A recovery topic given by the chairperson for group discussion
3. Small group check-ins.

The topic session by the chair is a thirty or more minute time where the group dialogues about a recovery topic. The small group check-in is where two or three partners pair off, talk about how they really are doing, and what is going on in their life. This way each member really gets to share fully how it has been going, and asks for feedback from the other one or two members of the group.

This type of small group allows everyone to have time instead of the one partner who is in the most pain dominating the other group members time. This seems to work really well and helps the group meet each others needs. During this small group check-in, the person who is sharing can ask for feedback, and receive the strength and hope she needs, along with some positive tips from others.

If there is not a Partners Group in your local area, feel free to start one. You don't need to be a professional, just be willing to be available. If you call our office, we can direct you to the groups we know about. If there isn't one, you might need to be the one to start it. If you do start a Partner's Group, please notify our office. If you want us to put it in our newsletter, (via e-mail) that goes out weekly to thousands of partners, we may be able to do this as well. For more information call (719)-278-3708 or e-mail us at heart2heart@xc.org.

Now I also realize that some of you reading this book are quite a distance away from a major metropolitan area. The internet is growing in its resources to partners of sex addicts. On our website we have links to on-line support groups on our links page at www.sexaddict.com and a religious support group, under our religious links page.

No matter what kind of group you participate in, I believe a group of some type is definitely the way to expedite your healing from the affects of his sex addiction. The partners in these groups have been where you are, and they can further help you along in your recovery journey.

APPENDIX

APPENDIX A

SUPPORT GROUPS

Sex Addiction

Sex Addicts
Anonymous (SAA)
P.O. Box 70949
Houston, TX 77270
(713) 869-4902

Sexaholics Anonymous
P.O. Box 111910
Nashville, TN
37222-1910
(615) 331-6901

Sexual Compulsives
Anonymous (SCA)
Old Chelsea Station,
P.O. Box 1585
New York, NY
10013-0935
1-800-977-HEAL

Sex & Love Addicts
Anon., P.O. Box 119,
New Town Branch,
Boston, MA 02258
(617) 332-1845

Sexual Recovery
Anonymous (SRA),
PO Box 73,
Planetarium Station,
New York, NY 10024
(212) 340-4650 or:
PO Box 72044
Burnaby, BC V5H4PQ
Canada (604) 290-9382

Freedom Groups
Church-Based for Sex Addicts
P.O. Box 51055
Colorado Springs, CO 80907
(719) 278-3708

For the Partner or Family Member

COSA
P.O. Box 14537
Minneapolis, MN
55414
(612) 537-6904

S-Anon Intrntnl.
Family Groups
P.O. Box 111242
Nashville, TN
37222-1242
(615) 833-3152

Co-SLAA
P.O. Box 614
Brookline, MA
02146

Partners Groups
P.O. Box 51055
Colorado Springs, CO
80907
(719) 278-3708

Recovering Couples
Anonymous (RCA)
P.O. Box 11872
St. Louis, MO 63105
(314) 830-2600

Sexual Trauma Survivors

Survivors of Incest
Anonymous (SIA)
P.O. Box 21817
Baltimore, MD 21222
(410) 282-3400

Incest Survivors Anon.
P.O. Box 17245
Long Beach, CA 90807

Sexual Assault Recovery
Anonymous
P.O. Box 16
Surrey, British Columbia,
V35 424, Canada
(604) 584-2626

APPENDIX B

The Twelve Steps of Alcoholics Anonymous

1. We admitted we were powerless over alcohol--that our lives had become unmanageable.

2. Came to believe that a Power greater than ourselves could restore us to sanity.

3. Made a decision to turn our will and our lives over to the care of God as we understood Him.

4. Made a searching and fearless moral inventory of ourselves.

5. Admitted to God, to ourselves, and to another human being the exact nature of our wrongs.

6. Were entirely ready to have God remove all these defects of character.

7. Humbly asked Him to remove our shortcomings.

8. Made a list of all people we had harmed, and became willing to make amends to them all.

9. Made direct amends to such people wherever possible, except when to do so would injure them or others.

10. Continued to take personal inventory, and when we were wrong, promptly admitted it.

11. Sought through prayer and meditation to improve our conscious contact with God as we understood Him, praying only for knowledge of His will for us and the power to carry that out.

12. Having had a spiritual awakening as the result of these steps, we tried to carry this message to others and to practice these principles in all our affairs.

The Twelve Steps reprinted for adaptation by permission of AA World Services, Inc. Copyright 1939.

The Twelve Steps For Partners

1. We admitted we were powerless over our partners sexual addiction, and that our lives had become unmanageable.

2. Came to believe that a Power greater than ourselves could restore us to sanity.

3. Made a decision to turn our will and our lives over to the care of God as we understood Him.

4. Made a searching and fearless moral inventory of ourselves.

5. Admitted to God, to ourselves, and to another human being the exact nature of our wrongs.

6. Were entirely ready to have God remove all these defects of character.

7. Humbly asked Him to remove our shortcomings.

8. Made a list of all people we had harmed, and became willing to make amends to them all.

9. Made direct amends to such people wherever possible, except when to do so would injure them or others.

10. Continued to take personal inventory, and when we were wrong, promptly admitted it.

11. Sought through prayer and meditation to improve our conscious contact with God as we understood Him, praying only for knowledge of His will for us and the power to carry that out.

12. Having had a spiritual awakening as the result of these steps, we tried to carry this message to others and to practice these principles in all our affairs.

APPENDIX C
Material Descriptions

FOR PARTNERS

Now That I Know, What Should I Do?, **by Weiss--$69.95** This 90 minute video answers the ten most frequently asked questions by partners just finding out about their spouse's sexual addiction. The need for counseling is significantly reduced by listening to this video.

Sexual Anorexia, **by Weiss--90 min.Video $69.95** Sexual anorexia paralyzes those from having intimate relationships. This video will provide practical steps to stop withholding behaviors and begin intimacy in present and future relationships.

Beyond Love: 12 Step Recovery Guide for Partners, **by Weiss--$14.95** This is an interactive workbook that allows the partner to gain insight and strength through working the Twelve Steps. This book can be used individually or as a group step-study workbook.

Partners Recovery Guide, **by Weiss--$39.95** This is the most practical workbook for partners and was conceived from many years of successful treatment for partners of sex addicts. It includes 100 proven techniques used in counseling sessions to help partners.

How to Love When it Hurts So Bad, **by Weiss-- $38.00** This 4-tape audio series and workbook deals with the partner issues of an addict. This has a religious focus and gives biblical answers to boundaries, tough love, and how to love an addict the way God does.

FOR SEX ADDICTS

The Final Freedom: Pioneering Sexual Addiction Recovery, **by Weiss--Audio $35.00/Book $22.95** This five-audio-tape series/book gives more current information than many professional counselors have today. In addition to informing sex addicts and their partners about sex addiction, it gives hope for recovery. The information provided in this product would cost hundreds of dollars in counseling hours to receive. Many have attested to successful recovery from this product alone.

101 Practical Exercises for Sexual Addiction Recovery, **by Weiss-- $39.95** This workbook contains 101 proven techniques that Dr. Weiss has used to successfully help thousands obtain and maintain their sex addiction recovery. This is a great follow up tool for *The Final Freedom.*

101 Freedom Exercises: A Christian Guide for Sex Addiction Recovery, **by Weiss--$39.95** (Christian version of *101 Practical Exercises*)

Secret Solutions, by Weiss--Book $39.95 This workbook has over 100 practical exercises for the female sex addict. These exercises have been proven to be to be effective and is a must for any woman struggling with sexual addiction.

Steps of Hope: 12 Step Recovery Guide for Sex Addiction, **by Weiss--$14.95** This is a thorough interaction with the Twelve Steps of recovery. This workbook can be used in Twelve Step study groups, or individually.

Steps to Freedom: A Christian 12 Step Guide, **by Weiss--$14.95** (Christian version of *Steps of Hope*.)

She Has A Secret, by Weiss--Book $14.95 This book combines true stories of female sex addicts along with the most recent research on female sex addiction and understanding it.

FOR MARRIAGE/YOUTH

Intimacy; A 100 Day Guide, **by Weiss--$21.95** This 100 Day guide can transform a couple from any level of intimacy toward a deeper level. Dr. Weiss practically walks couples through the skills necessary to have a lifelong intimate relationship.

Pathways To Intimacy, by Weiss Robison, Evans--$35.00/5 Audios This audio series presents solutions to gaining intimacy in the marriage relationship. Nuggets of information are gleaned from national television host James Robison author Douglas Weiss, Ph.D. and Debra Evans. This is a great road map for couples wanting more out of their relationship.

Good Enough to Wait--by Weiss--$39.95 This 60 minute video is the Christian sex talk for teenagers for the 21st Century. Dr. Weiss combines the best scriptural teaching with a decade of research in the field of sexuality. This video comes with a commitment card (which researchers have found to profoundly increase the chances of waiting till marriage) and booklet. Youth Pastors in addition to parents will also greatly benefit from this video presentation.

ORDER FORM

Item	Quan	Price	Total

PARTNERS

Item	Quan	Price	Total
Now That I Know What Should I Do?	_____	$69.95	_____
Sexual Anorexia	_____	69.95	_____
Beyond Love	_____	14.95	_____
Partners; Healing From His Addiction	_____	14.95	_____
Partner's Recovery Guide	_____	39.95	_____
How To Love When It Hurts So Bad	_____	38.00	_____

SEX ADDICTS

Item	Quan	Price	Total
The Final Freedom-Book	_____	$22.95	_____
The Final Freedom-Audio	_____	35.00	_____
*101 **Practical** Exercises*	_____	39.95	_____
*101 **Freedom** Exercises*	_____	39.95	_____
Secret Solutions	_____	39.95	_____
Steps of Hope	_____	14.95	_____
Steps to Freedom	_____	14.95	_____
She Has A Secret	_____	14.95	_____

MARRIAGE/YOUTH

Item	Quan	Price	Total
Intimacy	_____	$21.95	_____
Good Enough To Wait	_____	39.95	_____
Pathways To Intimacy	_____	35.00	_____

Sub Total _____

6.1 % Sales Tax (in CO only) _____

Shipping: $5 + .50 ea. addtl. item (in USA) _____

Outside USA: $10 + $1 for ea. addtl. item _____

Total _____

To order: 719-278-3708

VISA/MC/DISCOVER #_____ EXP DATE ____

NAME _____ SIGNATURE _____

ADDRESS _____ CITY _____

STATE ___ ZIP CODE _____ PHONE (_____)_____

OR MAIL TO: Heart to Heart Counseling Center,

P.O. Box 51055, Colorado Springs, CO 80949

OR E-MAIL TO: heart2heart@xc.org

(Make Checks payable to Heart to Heart Counseling Center)

3-DAY INTENSIVE SCHEDULE
for 2001-2002
with Douglas Weiss, Ph.D.
Colorado Springs, CO

Our 3-Day Intensive workshops are a huge success. Couples receive 3 sessions (individuals 2 sessions) each day of personal counseling with Dr. Weiss. Support groups are available during the evening. The following are 2001-2002 Intensive dates.

2001 Intensive Dates

January 2-4, 8-10, 15-17, 22-24, 29-31
February 5-7, 12-14, 19-21, 26-28
March 5-7, 12-14, 19-21, 26-28
April 2-4, 9-11, 16-18, 23-25, 30-May 2
May 7-9, 14-16, 21-23, 29-31
June 4-6, 11-13, 18-20, 25-27
July 9-11, 16-18, 23-25, 30-Aug. 1
August 6-8, 13-15, 20-22, 27-29
September 4-6, 10-12, 17-19, 24-26
October 1-3, 8-10, 15-17, 22-24, 29-31
November 5-7, 12-14, 19-21, 26-28
December 3-5, 10-12, 17-19

2002 Intensive Dates

January 7-9, 14-16, 21-23, 28-30
February 4-6, 11-13, 18-20, 25-27
March 4-6, 11-13, 18-20, 25-27
April 1-3, 8-10, 15-17, 22-24
May 6-8, 13-15, 20-22, 27-29
June 3-5, 10-12, 17-19, 24-26
July 1-3, 8-10, 15-17, 22-24, 29-31
August 5-7, 12-14, 19-21, 26-28
September 2-4, 9-11, 16-18, 23-25
October 7-9, 14-16, 21-23, 28-30
November 4-6, 11-13, 18-20, 25-27
December 2-4, 9-11, 16-18, 23-25

Availability limited.

Cost: $950/Individual Pre-paid*
$1,200/Couple Pre-paid*
(MC, Visa, Discover, & American Express accepted)
*Does not include travel, lodging, or meals

Here's what our attendees had to say!

100%   Attendees responded that they felt their intensive was "Very Helpful."

100%   Believed their marriage has improved "greatly."

100%   Stated they would recommend this Intensive to others.

81%   Maintained complete sobriety. (19% had a couple slips, but still are actively on the road to sobriety.

"Everything you said to us in those 3 days was so right and so healing! I felt like a big load was taken off my back while counseling with you!"

"Thanks to Dr. Doug we're not only <u>not</u> getting divorced we're actually sober & still in love."

"Without the intensive, my marriage would have ended and I would not have known why. Now I am happier than ever and my marriage is bonded permanently."

"The 3-Day Intensive gave me the help I really needed...Our marriage could not have survived without this Intensive."

"Dr. Weiss, I can't thank you enough. Our marriage is better than ever thanks to you and the sessions. Keep up the great work!"

"I was unsure as to whether or not I would still have a marriage when I arrived. After the 3-Day Intensive, I became stronger myself upon implementation of Dr. Weiss's recommendations. Myself, my husband and our relationship has done nothing but grow. He gave me tools to use that helped me come out of "emergency" mode and allowed me to bring sanity back into my life with confidence. Thank you Dr. Doug!"

"I can not begin to thank you enough for all that you have done for me and my husband...I am continually getting stronger every day and thinking clearly again."

"I would encourage other women to attend a 3-Day Intensive with Dr. Weiss. Dr. Weiss is one of the few people that addresses the partner's recovery."

"I applaud you for spending your time working with these people and with us...Thanks for your help in our lives."

"I've thanked God (everyday since we've been there) for leading us to you! I feel like shouting your name & phone number to the whole world!"

TELEPHONE COUNSELING
with
author/therapist
DOUGLAS WEISS, Ph.D.

Dear Reader,

We are happy to introduce you to the opportunity of telephone counseling with Dr. Douglas Weiss at Heart to Heart Counseling Center. Counseling is provided for those having issues with sexual addiction, partner's or sexual anorexia issues. As you work through this workbook, and you have some concerns or issues you would like professional help with, call Heart to Heart Counseling Center. All telephone counseling is strictly confidential.

To schedule a telephone appointment with Dr. Weiss, **call 719-278-3708**. When you call to schedule your appointment, you will be given a **toll-free number** (within USA). Call the toll-free number at the time of your scheduled appointment. We will need 24 hours notice for changes in appointments or cancellations otherwise you will be billed for your appointment.

Counseling costs are $125 per hour. We accept Mastercard, VISA, or Discover, or American Express. We look forward to hearing from you.

BEST PORN BLOCKER ON THE WEB

Don't worry about relapsing on the net!

**This porn blocker will block
porn, newsgroup, etc.**

Once you download this from our webpage

www.SEXADDICT.com

you can't get rid of it for a year.

**There are no parental controls or passwords
(which means you can't get around it,
or delete it) just smooth, clean
sailing on the internet.**

**I waited for years for the right Blocker
that anyone can use and afford
at $36 a year.**

**The block is checked daily and is run by a
nonprofit organization that has been
protesting Porn for over 20 years.**

**Just go to our site and click where you see
the little blue ball!**